SKITS

THAT TEACH

Adults

Colleen Ison

"And let us consider
how we may spur one another on
toward love and good deeds."
—Hebrews 10:24

Skits That Teach Adults is a revision
of *Skits That Teach*

**STANDARD
PUBLISHING**
Cincinnati, Ohio

The Standard Publishing Company, Cincinnati, Ohio
A division of Standex International Corporation
Revised ©1993 by The Standard Publishing Company
All rights reserved
Printed in the United States of America

00 99 98   5 4 3

Ison, Colleen, 1962-
    Skits that teach adults : including "Tell the truth" and 11
other short dramas / by Colleen Ison.
    p. ; cm.
    ISBN 0-87403-949-5
    1. Drama in Christian education. 2. Christian drama,
American. 3. Christian education of adults. 4. Amateur
plays. I. Title.
BV1534.4.I863   1993
268'.434--dc20   93-315
                                                    CIP

Foreword

Plays are exciting. Being in a play fills people with that mixture of joy, anticipation and terror which tends to bring out the best in them. By performing in even the simplest of skits they learn to overcome fear, to speak confidently in public, and to communicate powerfully.

Best of all, the process of rehearsal and preparation builds unity. Working toward a short-term goal will bring people together faster than anything else. When that goal is a relevant play about Christian life, the benefits are doubled. When the play is then performed for others, the benefits multiply.

When people come to a play they come with hope and expectation. They want to be moved to laugh, or cry, or learn something that changes things for them. When Christians weave drama into the life of the church, good things happen.

It is my hope that this book will be a well-used resource in the life of your church.

God bless your theatrical efforts, big and small.

—Colleen Ison

How to Use These Skits

You will probably think of many other ways to use these skits and discussion questions and many situations where they will be applicable. Here are a few suggestions.

—Use the skits for mid-week services, monthly men's and women's meetings, or home Bible studies. These small groups are perfect settings for the discussion to follow.
—Let adults present a skit for the youth group hour.
—The innovative minister might use a skit to introduce his sermon topic.
—Make copies of the page of questions and distribute them to everyone.
—Hand out one question each to several good discussion leaders.
—Set up a panel of "experts."
—Set up a debate between parents and youth, men and women, church leaders and lay people.
—Send the questions home as written assignments. either for personal study or to be discussed the following week.

For any of the skits, you can arrange a full-blown production with memorized lines, props, and scenery, or do a "reader's theater" type of presentation where your characters read (after practice) their parts.

Tips for Directors

—Allow enough time for rehearsal.

—Lines should be memorized early on in the rehearsal process. Rehearsal is not for the purpose of learning lines, but for the practice of movement and delivery and work on character. These things cannot really be done with actors who are tied to scripts. Require actors to be off-script early on in the process. After your deadline, forbid scripts on stage. For anyone having memory trouble, appoint a "prompt," to follow rehearsal on a script and supply the needed line, but only when the actor asks for it.

—Suggest that people having trouble learning lines work on them with partners reading all the other characters for them. They could also record the piece on a cassette tape, reading everyone's lines but their own, leaving enough space for them to say their lines with the tape. Remember that cues as well as lines must be memorized. Tell actors you will not have a prompt for the performance. This is a great incentive to memorize.

—A rehearsal tip: Videotape a rehearsal to let actors see themselves. It's worth a thousand director's words.

—Be affirming. This is so important. People need frequent praise to grow in confidence. Affirmation offsets the tediousness of rehearsal's repetition, and softens your frequent demands that they speak up, slow down, move differently, etc. You will get a great deal more spontaneity and energy from the actors if you praise often and request changes without criticism.

—Audibility: Do not allow very much rehearsal below required volume. It reinforces the bad habit. Call for louder voices as much as it takes, which will be a lot. Remember that very few people are physically incapable of projecting. They just need to become comfortable with hearing their own voices at high volume.

—Visibility: Block plays so that actors never need to deliver lines with their backs to the audience. Always correct actors if they do this. Groups need to open out into horseshoes, actors stand on a diagonal that leaves them open to the audience when they are talking to each other, tall people move behind short people, etc.

—Timing: Pay attention to the pace of speech and action. People speed up when they are nervous. Break them of this early on by requiring repetition of lines until they slow down. Another timing problem with new actors is that they take too long to pick up cues, particularly when they are supposed to interrupt. The skill that overcomes this is listening. If they listen deeply to their cues, their responses will have more natural timing.

—Prohibit put-downs in rehearsal. They are very destructive.

—Be clear about who's directing. To avoid too many chiefs, suggest that anyone with a directing idea suggest it quietly to the director rather than delivering it themselves. This also protects struggling performers from getting too much advice.

—Along with tons of praise, set high expectations for the cast. They will usually meet them.

—Most important of all, have fun!

Contents

Seven Steps
to Silence Christians

People who reject Christ will go to Hell after they die. That is a fact we prefer not to think about. But if we don't think about it, we won't do anything about it, and those who would have heard of Christ through us will not be saved.

This skit reveals the excuses we use to keep from witnessing to those we are in daily contact with. It revolves around a conversation between two demons (acknowledgements to C.S. Lewis) who are observing Christians in everyday situations. One demon is using the situations to illustrate ways to prevent witnessing. He is teaching the other demon, who is a beginner in the art.

They will remain to one side of the stage, observing the thoughts and actions of the humans on center stage. If possible, elevate them on a small platform to enable them to look down on the rest of the action.

There is no scenery, and the only props are items that people carry on and off stage with them.

Characters

The Demons—should be played by two sharp-looking young men wearing three piece suits or sophisticated clothes. Their manner should be cool, intelligent, and professional. Any reference to God is made with complete sincerity—they know how great His power is. This image, combined with the cruelty of what they are saying, will be more convincingly evil than any attempt to create non-human demons.

Ashley—The more experienced demon, has more lines than Bernard, but both should be excellent actors. Their conversation must flow smoothly and naturally, because their dialogue makes up most of the skit.

Humans—Three workmen; two young women; a teenage girl and a boy and a group of ten other teenagers; a teenage girl or young woman; a group of five people of varied ages.

(Ashley and Bernard enter, engaged in conversation, and take up the positions they will hold throughout the skit.)

ASHLEY: Now that you've been promoted from the Starvation Strategies Department, what's your new assignment?

BERNARD: Well, actually, that's what I wanted to talk to you about, Ashley. I'm working in your area now.

ASHLEY: Is that a fact? Well, welcome to the crew. I think you'll find it a challenge. Witnessing Prevention will test the creative capacities of any demon. He must be pleased with you to put you with us. He considers it the most vital area in our whole campaign.

BERNARD *(with false modesty)*: Well, he did say I have potential! But I'll level with you, Ashley. This is a whole new game for me. I hardly know where to start.

ASHLEY: Want me to give you a few tips?

BERNARD: Oh, would you? I certainly would be grateful.

ASHLEY: Sure. After all, we're in this together, and we have a common goal. We demons compete with each other too much. We should worry about our positions in the hierarchy *after* we destroy the humans, not before. Don't you agree, Bernard?

BERNARD: Certainly. A very good point.

Ashley: OK. Now I will tell you something that is going to make your job a great deal easier—there are just seven things that you must keep Christians from realizing. If you can't stop them from believing in these ideas, just make sure they keep them in the back of their minds out of danger of being acted on.

BERNARD: Just seven things?

ASHLEY: Yes, I'll bet you can guess the first one from watching this.

(Ashley gestures toward the stage as three workmen carrying lunch boxes enter, two from the left, one from the right. The two together are laughing and boisterous. The one by himself looks a little sheepish.)

ASHLEY *(points to the single man)*: Pay attention to the Christian.

MAN 1 *(with ridicule in his voice)*: Hi Mike.

MAN 3: Hi Fred, hi Stan.

(They pass, but Man 2 calls back to Man 3, who stops.)

MAN 2: Hey Mike!

MAN 3: Yeah?

MAN 2: Are you absolutely sure that the world's going to end with a trumpet blast and Jesus is going to zap in through the clouds and I am going to be thrown in the lake of fire? *(He and Man 1 laugh uproariously.)*

(Man 3 bows his head and says nothing.)

MAN 1: Hey, Mike, I don't see you carrying around your New Testament lately. Had some second thoughts?

(They continue laughing as they exit. Man 3 exits with his head bowed.)

ASHLEY: This is a very pleasing situation—a good example of the success I am having in applying point number one. When that guy Mike started working in this machine shop, he was a real threat. During lunch breaks, he started talking to the other men about the Enemy, and some of them became so interested that he started bringing his Bible in. I mean he was actually reading it to about twelve guys who'd never heard it before. The situation was degenerating so fast I had to call in a task force of three of the best demons we've got. They set to work on some of the strongest personalities in the place and got them to make fun of the ones who were interested. One of the demons had a brilliant flash and gave the foreman the idea to grab the Bible from Mike and read sections out of context. In an instant, that had everyone thinking Mike was a lunatic, all the interest was squelched and he's been afraid to speak since!

BERNARD: Ridicule is that powerful?

ASHLEY: It certainly is, Bernard. Point number one: subject the witnessing Christian to ridicule and the inactive Christian to fear of ridicule. In most cases you can nip witnessing—or the desire to witness—in the bud before any real harm is done.

BERNARD: Great. What's the next point?

ASHLEY: Watch again.

(Two well-dressed young women enter from left and stop at center stage. One is very confident, more flamboyantly dressed, and carries a briefcase. Girl 2 is obviously impressed with the more outgoing girl.)

GIRL 2: That story you did on the modern dance company was fantastic! I like the way you centered it on the personalities of the principals.

GIRL 1: Thanks. It was fun to do. They're having a party tonight and they've invited me.

GIRL 2: Really? That's great. They must have liked your story too!

GIRL 1: Well, what are you doing this weekend, Karen?

GIRL 2: Uh, tomorrow I'm going water skiing, and on Sunday our church is having a special service—there's going to be some good musicians and a visiting speaker. Uh, you're welcome to come if you want to. *(She is a bit hesitant)* You know, it's the sort of thing a lot of visitors come to.

GIRL 1: Oh thanks. It sounds great, but I've got so much going on already. The party tonight, a lunch date tomorrow, then another party tomorrow night—I think I'd better reserve Sunday to relax!

GIRL 2: Oh sure. I understand.

(Ashley resumes speaking as the girls exit right, still looking as though they are talking.)

ASHLEY: Now the Christian admires the other girl to no end—thinks she's got it all—talent, looks, personality, popularity. She is a mature Christian and her conscience keeps telling her to share the gospel with her friend, but she never gets anywhere because we have her convinced that this girl has everything and feels no need of the Enemy, so she feels defeated before she starts.

BERNARD: Ah—so we prevent the Christian from seeing the heart!

ASHLEY: You catch on quickly. Most people project an image of well-being to their acquaintances; our task is to persuade Christians to believe it. The really ironic thing about this particular case is that Karen's friend is absolutely despairing—she is totally disillusioned.

BERNARD *(smiling):* Is that so?

ASHLEY *(grinning):* She's contemplating suicide! Unless something unforeseen happens, we'll have her in a matter of weeks.

BERNARD *(regarding Ashley with admiration):* Well done, Ashley.

ASHLEY: Thank you. Now, closely related to keeping the Christian unaware of people's needs is point number three: keep the Christian feeling ill-equipped to meet those needs. When you do come across the rare Christian who has been corrupted to the point that he is utterly convinced of everyone's need of Christ, make him feel he hasn't the knowledge or the right words to communicate his faith!

(About a dozen people enter, all holding a glass and talking in small groups. They are having a party. The Christian in the party is standing a little separate, towards the front of the stage, talking to a girl.)

ASHLEY: See the Christian there talking to the girl? He's a new Christian—sickeningly devout. Bible study, praise, confession, intercession, active service—the whole show. But, he won't open his mouth to talk about the Enemy with his non-believing friends! Thinks he doesn't know enough about the Bible yet—he's afraid he'll mess up, thanks to us. Listen.

GIRL: So what have you been doing lately? I don't see much of you anymore.

CHRISTIAN: Well, I've been pretty busy lately. Taken up a few new interests.

GIRL: Oh yeah? What?

CHRISTIAN: Uh, well, I'm involved with a church.

GIRL: You? A church?

CHRISTIAN: Yeah.

GIRL: Why are you involved in a church? You never used to care about stuff like that.

CHRISTIAN *(with much difficulty):* Well, I've become a, a Christian.

GIRL *(very interested):* This is unbelievable! How did all this come about?

CHRISTIAN: Well, I just decided I needed to make a few changes. *(Abruptly.)* How about you? What have you been doing?

(They continue their conversation inaudibly, and the whole party begins exiting right.)

BERNARD *(laughs):* Exquisite! He blew the most perfect opportunity! She was genuinely interested and he didn't dare say a thing!

ASHLEY *(smiling):* He does it all the time! Keep this point in mind with new converts especially. New converts are often dangerous. They are enthusiastic and have many friends who are unbelievers. If you can keep them feeling insecure about communicating their faith for a few years, it will give us time to wean them away from the friends who need them most.

(A girl enters and stands looking up, an intense, searching expression on her face.)

BERNARD *(looking at her with interest):* She looks good and miserable. What's her problem?

ASHLEY: Oh that one. Her kind gives me special delight. The Christian perpetually seeking guidance! So much wasted potential! We have persuaded her to treat the Enemy as a sort of crystal ball—she peers up at the heavens waiting for the Lord's will to be revealed to her in a clear vision!

BERNARD: I don't understand. How does that keep her from witnessing?

ASHLEY: Simple, my friend, She is so preoccupied with the future, it renders her totally ineffectual for the present! Until she hears a voice from Heaven directing her to some far-away mission field, she doesn't really feel that her service has begun. She doesn't see the opportunities that come up in her everyday life.

BERNARD: What a laugh! Oblivious to the needs under her nose. How much time does she spend standing there like that, beseeching the heavens?

ASHLEY: Oh lots. It eats up most of the time she sets aside for devotions and a lot of time she should be studying or spending with people. Our aim is to keep her deluded about the nature of the Enemy's guidance until she gives up, thinking He is neglecting her by offering no clear direction. Keep her at bay, steer her away from action for as long as possible. You can allow her to accumulate knowledge about people's needs, but whatever you do, don't let her get involved! If she gets involved in something—anything really—the possibilities are horrifying because this type is very loyal and conscientious once committed.

BERNARD: I see.

ASHLEY: The next point should give you a lot of amusement. You should *encourage* evangelism programs.

BERNARD *(shocked):* Encourage evangelism?

ASHLEY: That's not what I said. I said encourage programs. Not the actual reaching out to friends and neighbors, but programs that become the *end* not the *means.* Look at this group. Observe their intense excitement.

(Five people rush on stage—one holding a map with circles and dots all over it. Two people stand to each side of him once they reach center stage, each leaning in excitedly, looking at the map, but their bodies still face the audience. They point to the map, gesture wildly, mime animated conversation. This continues as the demons resume talking.)

BERNARD: What are they doing?

ASHLEY *(smiling):* They are planning a strategy for neighborhood Bible studies in church members' homes and advertised by a doorknock—as well as an extensive follow-up program for the non-members who attend.

BERNARD: Sounds frightening. Why are you smiling?

ASHLEY: Because they are never going to do it! This is their fifth meeting and they are no closer to starting than they were at the first! They're feeling elated because they were successful in getting funds for the literature they want. And they have secured the elders' approval and have been allocated a community outreach fund in the church's budget. That's enough for them at the moment. If we keep them talking long enough, they'll get sick of the whole idea before it ever gets off the ground. Meanwhile, everyone else in the church feels they don't need to do much witnessing because they have an evangelism committee to take care of it.

BERNARD: That's wonderful! Diabolical!

ASHLEY: Think big, Bernard. It is best when you can mastermind strategies that affect a whole church. It is a better use of our time and energy than handling individuals separately. You know how much influence these fools have over one another.

BERNARD *(nods):* So let me review. *(Checks each point off on his fingers.)* I instill a fear of ridicule, a belief that people are happy and have no need of the Enemy, a sense of inability to communicate the gospel, a preoccupation with the future, and diversion from people to programs.

ASHLEY: Very good.

BERNARD: But that's only five. I thought you mentioned seven.

ASHLEY: I did. I saved the most important two for last. One seems too simple to warrant mentioning, but it must always be kept in mind: don't let them talk about Hell, or death, which leads to discussion about Hell. Distract the preachers from it, persuade the teachers to shy away from it, keep the theologians and writers from dealing with it. *(He becomes subdued.)* You know as well as I do that if they caught one glimpse of it, they would be beyond all our devices. . . . *(Resumes former manner)* So, use your imagination. See how many different types of trivia you can submerge them in to prevent them from addressing weighty issues.

BERNARD *(with relish):* You mean pull them down with drugs and alcohol and perversion?

ASHLEY *(shrugs):* If you wish. But that's a little too obvious to be successful with most church people. Trip them up on the acceptable things. Get them addicted to TV, or absorbed in improving their homes, or preoccupied with food. It's fun to see them stumbling over the obvious. Just tie them up in the routine matters of their personal world. Hell will seem very far away.

BERNARD: And what is the last point, Ashley?

ASHLEY *(with conviction):* Bernard, whatever you do or fail to do, do not let them realize the power of the Enemy.

BERNARD: I understand you. That applies in every area of the strategy. We must keep them from praying.

ASHLEY *(winces):* I hate that word. But yes, don't let them learn to—truly—pray. They can mutter benedictions or spout cliches during their meetings, but keep them from individual and small-group prayer. If they learn to pray, they can ask for courage and opportunities to witness. Both will be granted, and before long they will become unmanageably bold. We can lose thousands—perhaps millions. *(Both demons slowly shake their heads at the thought.)* So Bernard, if you remember these things, you will have success.

BERNARD: Ashley, I don't know how to thank you for your advice. You have saved me months of learning.

ASHLEY: Then let's both get to work. The time is running short.

(They exit.)

Questions for Discussion

1. What were the seven points that hinder a Christian's witness?

2. Can you give examples of any of these from your own life?

3. What are some of the most difficult situations in which to witness?

4. Can you give any examples of a time in which it was difficult for you to witness, but you went ahead anyway? What was the reaction of the person or persons you were trying to reach?

5. Can you recall a time when you saw a prayer answered in a witnessing situation? That is, you saw the connection between prayer and effective witnessing?

6. How can programs and strategies get in the way of our being the kind of witness we should be?

7. What qualities make a Christian a positive witness for Christ?

8. What can we do to help one another to be more effective witnesses?

9. There seems to be a gap between knowing something to be true (a promise from God, for example), and believing it to the point of acting on it. How can we cross this gap? How would our behavior change if we actually believed our unsaved friends were going to Hell? How would our behavior change if we actually believed that God, through the Holy Spirit, would change our timidity to power (2 Timothy 1:7)?

Matters of Necessity

Throughout the Bible there is a clear emphasis on the need to care for the poor, but the whole issue is one that many Christians prefer not to think about. In a society as materialistic as ours, we need to be reminded of the difference between needs and wants, and of what we are doing when we allow ourselves to have too much.

This skit has seven characters, three poor people, three average people and a mediator. A poor person states a need to the audience, an average person states a want, the mediator points out the poor person's need, and the average person gives an excuse for ignoring that need.

Characters

Poor people—a young woman, an old woman, a middle aged man.

Average people—a businessman, a teenage girl, an old man.

Mediator—a person casually dressed, looking neither rich nor poor.

(Three poor people are lined up on one side of the stage, with the average people lined up on the other side of the stage. They are all several feet apart from one another. The mediator is standing in the center. The characters will have nothing to do with one another, addressing only the audience, and the mediator.)

YOUNG POOR WOMAN: I don't know what I'm going to do. My rent has just been raised by $30 a month, but welfare's not going up just because the rent went up. I'm really stuck. I can't work—I have a baby. And there isn't any cheaper place to live—I'm in a government subsidized apartment now. I just don't know what I'm going to do.

(She takes a step backwards, lowers her head and remains in that position for the rest of the play.)

BUSINESSMAN: Well that last raise set me up pretty well. I think I can afford to start investing a little more each month. Not much—I'm no big wheel on the stock market, but I do think I could start playing around with an extra $200 or so a month. Yeah. I'll do that.

MEDIATOR *(politely):* Uh, excuse me. I couldn't help but over-hear your plan to invest more money, and I thought I might just point out to you that there's a girl over here who's really stuck. She needs an extra $30 a month or she'll be evicted from her apartment, and she doesn't have anywhere else to go! I don't want to pry into your personal affairs, but I was wondering if, objectively speaking, it wouldn't make an awful lot of sense to invest, say, $170 or so, and give her $30 each month?

BUSINESSMAN: Where's her husband?

MEDIATOR: Well, I don't know that she has one.

BUSINESSMAN: Well, she shouldn't have gotten herself into that predicament. Am I supposed to pick up the tab for her immorality? Let her suffer the consequences. *(Picking up an imaginary phone.)* Hello, Diane? Get me Gerald Henderson, my investment counselor, please.

(Mediator looks disappointed. The businessman, still holding the imaginary telephone, takes a step backward and remains in that position for the rest of the skit.)

OLD POOR WOMAN: I'm so tired of being cold! I've got sweaters and coats from the Salvation Army, but my bedroom has so many drafts I need a heater and some good blankets. Some slippers would be nice, too. And I'd love to buy some new shoes—some with good thick soles that wouldn't get holes in them too fast.

YOUNG GIRL *(pretending to look at something in a store)*: Ooooh! Look at this sweater! *(Pretends to pick up sweater, hold it up to herself and look at it.)* Oh wow! It's so gorgeous . . . oh I shouldn't really. I already did all my winter shopping. But this is just so beautiful . . . How much is it? *(Pretends to pick up a sleeve and look at the price tag.)* $150 . . . Well, it is expensive but—I want it. I'll just spend less than I planned on my new ski suit.

MEDIATOR *(taking a few steps toward her from his central position)*: Excuse me—I know this isn't any of my business, and that is a terrific sweater, but it's just that I heard an old lady over there *(Points.)* say how cold she is and how she needs some basic things like blankets and shoes, and I couldn't help thinking that $150 could really help her through the winter, and as you said, you don't really *need* the sweater. . . .

YOUNG GIRL *(interrupting)*: Well what does that have to do with me? I mean, this isn't my money anyway. This money's a present from my grandparents. They told me to buy stuff for myself with it.

MEDIATOR *(appealing)*: Does it matter? The old lady's got cold feet and you've got $150.

YOUNG GIRL *(getting upset)*: Come off it! What are you picking on me for? There are charities to take care of people like that! What am I supposed to do? Carry around the problems of the world? I'm just a kid. *(She tosses her head and says to an imaginary saleslady.)* I'll take this please. *(Pretends to hand sweater over.)* Cash.

(She takes a step backward, crosses her arms, and holds her head high. She remains in that position for the rest of the skit.)

(Mediator returns to his position, shaking his head.)

MEDIATOR: This is ridiculous.

POOR MAN *(spreads his arms wide in a gesture of helplessness):* I lost my job. They closed the whole plant. I worked there twenty years, then nothing. Suddenly I've got no job, but still have a wife and four kids to support. My friend Bill's boss says he can take on another guy next month, but that's four weeks away. I've got exactly $15 in my wallet—how am I going to make it till then? Some red tape hassle with the welfare people means I have to wait to get unemployment benefits, so I just don't know what to do. I never thought this would happen to me.

(He takes a step backward, bows his head and remains in that position for the rest of the skit.)

MATURE MAN: Ah, it's great to be retired. I'm having the time of my life. I just got back from Florida—the wife and I have been there since Christmas. This summer, we are going on one of those European tours—we've always wanted to do that. Anyway, today I'm shopping—looking at furniture. We're finally getting rid of the old stuff.

MEDIATOR *(walking up to him):* Pardon me, Sir, but I am really disturbed by the predicament of a man over there. *(Points.)* He just lost his job.

MATURE MAN: Hey, that's too bad. I know what he's going through. I was out of work in '72.

MEDIATOR: Well, he is getting another job in a month . . .

MATURE MAN: Good!

MEDIATOR: . . . but that's four weeks away, and he's flat broke with a big family to feed. He doesn't seem to have anyone who can help him out. I guess I was wondering if you could see your way clear to helping him out, since you seem to be doing all right financially?

MATURE MAN (patronizingly): Son, if your heart bleeds for every unlucky guy in the world, there soon won't be anything left of you. No, every man has to take care of himself. I managed in the hard times somehow—he will too. We all have our bad times and our good times. Besides, I'm retired. (Jabs his finger at mediator for emphasis.) When you no longer have an income you have to be careful what you do with your money! Hey! (Looks past the mediator, pointing further beyond.) I like that recliner! Real leather!

(Still looking at the recliner with a smile on his face, he takes a step backward and remains in that position.)

MEDIATOR (walking back to his central position): This is unbelievable. It would have barely dented their pocketbooks (Points to the average folks.) to make a huge difference in their lives. (Points to the poor.)

Questions for Discussion

1. What were the excuses in this skit for ignoring the needs of the poor? What are some other common excuses?

2. How do you define what is a need and what is a want? How can our perspective of material things become distorted?

3. In addition to immorality, what caused Sodom's downfall? See Ezekiel 16:49.

4. What does Matthew 25:34-46 tell us about the ultimate importance of caring for those in need?

5. Is giving possessions and money always the best way to help the needy? When might it be harmful? What could be an alternative?

6. Would a person of any income level feel welcomed and accepted into our church? How can we break down the social separation that often occurs between "haves" and "have-nots"?

7. What is the world's definition of wealthy? What is a Christian definition of wealth?

8. Whether or not you consider yourself wealthy is a matter of comparison. When you consider that 35,000 people die every day from hunger related causes,* are you wealthy?

*Statistic from 1982 study by The Hunger Project, San Francisco, CA.

Tell the Truth

This skit deals with hypocrisy in the church—our tendency to make ourselves look good but do nothing about the sins that take place in our minds.

Members of the Average Christian Church are exposed to the "truth testing" machine on a "Candid Camera" type of television show and all their thoughts are revealed.

The only props required are a "truth testing" device (a long thin object that can be pointed, decorated to look interesting), and a sign on the back wall reading "Average Christian Church." The setting is the outside of the church building after the service. If you wish, the left side of your stage may be made to look like the outside of a church door, through which characters will come on stage.

Characters

Compere—Very obnoxious, loud, sleazy man wearing a bright-colored suit and clashing tie.

Rhonda—His flashily dressed female sidekick. She never speaks, but smiles and looks sexy for the skit's duration.

Church members—An old man, two teenage girls, a young man, a woman of any age, a middle-aged couple.

(Compere enters right, bounds on stage holding a micro-phone, jumps to a halt at center stage, spreads his arms wide, smiles expansively.)

COMPERE: Good evening, good evening, good evening, and welcome to another revealing episode of "Tell the Truth."

All our regular viewers will remember what fun we had last week when we zeroed our truth tester in on some federal election candidates. Now this week, we have something a little different for you.

We thought we'd pay a visit to some of our friends at the Average Christian Church, to see how the good people there are progressing on their pilgrimage to paradise.

We'll be talking briefly with some of the folks as they leave after the morning service, and we'll let the truth tester tell us if their words are matching the intentions of their hearts!

Are these Christians really any different from the rest of us? We'll find out! Yes, no one escapes the effects of our magi-cal machine, that revolutionary gadget that will forevermore strip men of the privacy of their inner sentiments! We mere-ly point it in a person's direction, activate it, and the victim unwittingly spills exactly what is going on in his or her mind!

But first, let's welcome our truth tester operator to the show. Heeeeeere's Rhonda!

(Rhonda enters, wearing a glittery dress, holding a device labeled "Truth Tester." She stands to the right of Compere, smiles and holds the truth tester up for a few seconds.)

COMPERE: Hello, Rhonda. I see you have our trusty truth tester safely in your possession. That means we're ready to begin. And it sounds like our first victim—I mean guest—is coming in now!

(An older man walks out of the church entrance, and proceeds across the stage. Compere intercepts him near center stage.)

COMPERE: Excuse me, Sir. We're from "Tell the Truth" and we were wondering if you could tell us what you thought of the sermon this morning.

OLD MAN: Oh, very encouraging indeed. I really found it most helpful. We have an enthusiastic young pastor, you know; really on the ball. His sermons are truly edifying.

(Rhonda creeps behind him and appears on the other side of the older man, without his awareness. She points truth tester at him and clicks it on. She follows this procedure for each victim, sometimes putting her finger to her lips to indicate for the audience to keep the secret.)

(The man leaps into a zombie like position, standing stiff and straight with his arms flattened to his sides. His eyes are wide and staring and he speaks as though hypnotized. This is the effect the truth tester will have on all victims.)

OLD MAN: Actually, I don't know who that silly young preacher thinks he is, spouting off his opinions week after week. He doesn't know half as much about the Bible as I do. If I were given the chance, I could do much better than he.

(Compere raises eyebrows and grins at the audience. Rhonda clicks off the truth tester, at which time the victim immediately resumes his former stance, unaware that anything has happened. Rhonda goes back to her former position. This procedure repeats itself with every victim.)

COMPERE: Thank you very much, Sir.

OLD MAN: No trouble at all.

(He exits. Two teenage girls enter. They are talking when Compere intercepts them.)

COMPERE: Pardon the interruption, girls. Could I ask you a few questions?

(Girls look self-conscious, look at the microphone, look at one another and giggle, then nod shyly.)

GIRL 1: OK.

COMPERE: Have you been attending church here for a long time?

GIRL 2: Yeah, our families have always come here.

COMPERE: And you usually sit together?

GIRL 1: Yes, We've been best friends for years.

COMPERE: Do you take part in any activities other than the services?

GIRL 1: Oh, yeah. We go to youth group every Sunday night and sometimes we do stuff on Saturdays like go bowling or clean windows for old people or something. We do a lot of different things.

COMPERE: So you enjoy taking part in these activities together?

GIRLS *(simultaneously)* : Oh, yes we love it. *(They smile at one another.)*

(Rhonda activates the truth tester on both of them at the same time. They assume zombie-like positions.)

GIRL 1: Well, I might love it if she wasn't such a selfish little flirt. She makes me so mad. Michael Anderson came over to sit next to *me* this morning and as soon as she saw him coming she grabbed the seat next to me so he would have to sit next to her. All she thinks about is boys, and she's usually most interested in the one who's interested in me!

(Remains zombie-like as Girl 2 speaks.)

GIRL 2: Honestly, church is such a drag. I feel like a bird in a cage in that place, especially with *her* hanging around me all the time, watching me like a hawk.

(Compere is delighted with these responses. He rubs his hands together gleefully.)

And I can't stand the activities, but I'd never tell anyone. I hate washing windows, bowling is a drag, the people here are all boring and those sermons get so old!

(Rhonda clicks off machine and resumes former position.)

COMPERE: Thanks for the little talk, girls.

GIRL 2: That's all right.

(They resume talking and exit right as a young man enters left.)

COMPERE: Quick, Rhonda, let's get this one. Excuse me, Sir. If I could just have a few minutes of your attention. We're making a television show on the attitudes of churchgoers . . .

YOUNG MAN: Oh yeah?

COMPERE: Could you tell me what is foremost in your mind when you leave a Sunday morning service?

YOUNG MAN *(pausing to think for a moment):* Uh, let's see. Generally I give some thought to the sermon—what was said and how I should apply it to my life, and I'm usually mulling over whether there is anything I can do during the week to help my brothers and sisters in the congregation.

(As he finishes speaking, Rhonda applies truth tester and he assumes zombie-like position.)

YOUNG MAN: Look, Pal, all I'm thinking about at the moment is what's at home cooking for Sunday lunch. Church is a nice thing to do, but I'm not going to let all the stuff they say in there get to me!

(Rhonda keeps the truth tester on the man, who remains still while Rhonda and Compere giggle and while Compere addressed the audience.)

COMPERE: Well, as you can see viewers, these good people are not what they appear to be!

(Rhonda removes truth tester and she and the young man resume their former position.)

COMPERE: Thanks very much. Your comment was most revealing.

YOUNG MAN: No problem. *(He exits.)*

COMPERE: This is more fun than I expected. Ready for the next one, Rhonda?

(Rhonda nods and smiles as a lady enters.)

COMPERE: Excuse me, Ma'am. We're from a television station, canvassing the attitudes of churchgoers. Could you tell us how you feel about the other worshipers in this congregation?

LADY: Oh, well, they're very kind. All the people are very friendly and I always feel as though they're interested in my well-being.

(Rhonda applies the truth tester. The woman assumes the zombie-like position.)

LADY: I could just scream when I walk out of this place. Everyone ignores me. All they ever say is, "How do you do" and "Isn't the weather nice." I've been here for three years and no one has ever asked me my opinion of anything, or whether I'd like to be involved in anything, or even invited me to Sunday lunch. If I got run over by a bus it would take them three months to realize I wasn't coming anymore!

(Compere shows surprise at the outburst, but still finds it amusing. Rhonda removes truth tester.)

COMPERE: Well thank you very much for speaking with us.

LADY: That's quite all right. *(She exits.)*

COMPERE: Time for one more interview!

(Middle-aged couple enters.)

COMPERE: Good morning to you both.

(Couple responds very warmly.)

HUSBAND: Morning, Sir.

WIFE: Good morning. How are you?

COMPERE: Just fine. I'm interviewing folks this morning for a TV show; exploring the attitudes of churchgoers. Could I ask you a few questions?

WIFE *(politely):* TV? What sort of show?

COMPERE *(a little flustered):* Oh, uh, well—a sort of current affairs program.

(The couple looks over at Rhonda, confused about where she fits in.)

COMPERE: And this is Rhonda, my, uh, technical assistant.

(The couple nods.)

HUSBAND: OK then, fire away!

COMPERE: How long have you been attending this church?

HUSBAND: Over twenty years. We're very involved. I'm an elder and my wife is a Sunday-school teacher. And we're both involved in several projects and committees.

COMPERE: I see. Sounds like the church demands a lot of your time.

WIFE: Yes, well, it does. But this work is so worthwhile, we enjoy it. I'm sure my husband agrees.

HUSBAND: I certainly do, dear. Nothing is more fulfilling or rewarding than the life of a couple involved in a vital, growing church, seeking together to live righteous lives.

COMPERE: Have you ever found that all this involvement eats up some of your leisure time, some of the time you need to relax?

HUSBAND: There is no time for sitting around when the Lord's work is waiting to be done. Marion and I don't think in terms of our own needs. Our priorities call us to service, isn't that right, Marion?

(Rhonda sneaks around into position and turns on truth tester. The husband and wife snap into zombie-like positions.)

WIFE: Are you kidding? *(Turns to Compere.)* Sometimes I just want to beg him to spend some time with me. We hardly get to talk anymore, or just do things like go for walks or see a movie. He's become very duty-bound over the years, very rigid and—predictable—we used to laugh a lot. We hardly ever laugh now.

HUSBAND: To be honest, church work has become an unbelievable burden lately. I was at a meeting every single night last week. They're all necessary meetings, but five in a row! By the last meeting I was fighting the strongest impulse to tear up all the committee reports on the table and run screaming from the church building.

(This causes Compere and Rhonda to burst out laughing. Rhonda clicks off truth tester and returns to her position as Compere thanks the couple.)

COMPERE: Thank you very much for your candid statements!

HUSBAND: Not at all. *(They exit.)*

COMPERE: And on that humorous note, ladies and gentlemen, we will conclude our show. It appears that these saintly folks have some attitudes not too different from us pagans after all! Maybe the only difference is that they don't want to admit them! Who knows what we would have come up with if we had tested the whole congregation? Perhaps a few shady business deals, or a pulpit take-over plot! Well, alas, our time has run out. Do join Rhonda and me next week for another load of laughs as we peek into the minds of our most respected citizens on "Tell the Truth." Bye now!

(They wave to audience and run off the stage.)

Questions for Discussion

1. Churchgoers are often called hypocrites. Is this label deserved?

2. Why did the churchgoers in this skit lie to the interviewer? Have you ever lied for a similar reason?

3. What would be a better way of reacting to a problem in the church than pretending the problem didn't exist?

4. Is it always necessary to tell the truth about everything? Is it hypocrisy to withhold the whole truth when asked about church affairs?

5. What are some examples of hypocrisy we should be aware of?

6. What must we do as individuals and as a church to encourage integrity and honesty in the way we deal with each other?

7. Besides saying one thing and meaning another, what other kinds of hypocrisy do we involve ourselves in?

8. What actions can the church as a whole take to help individual members be genuinely glad to participate in church activities?

How Did You Get to Be So Ungrateful?

This skit consists of an argument between a mother and daughter. The argument illustrates their lack of communication, the daughter's lack of respect and the mother's religious hypocrisy. This skit would be a good introduction to a discussion of family conflict.

The setting is a pleasant living room. To the right of the stage there is a table with a telephone on it and near the center of the stage is a couch and a chair or two.

Characters

Mother—conservative, churchy, very socially-minded, very image-conscious.

Daughter—a defensive, rebellious teenager.

(Mother is talking on the telephone.)

MOTHER: Mmn, yes Sylvia. I think we should hold a committee meeting soon so we can get the activities for the rest of the year planned. And I'll call Martha about the potluck dinner and see if the speaker is available for August.

(Daughter enters, drops school bag on the floor and throws herself into a chair.)

MOTHER: Oh yes, yes, I'll be happy to have the next meeting here. After all, we had the extension built so that we could hold more church functions here, and anyway, just between you and me, I've completely redecorated and I'm just dying to show it off to someone! *(Laughs.)*

(Daughter rolls her eyes.)

MOTHER: Listen, where should we hold the meeting after that? I mean, I know it's scheduled for Ruth's house but I really have my doubts about whether we should have it there again. You remember last time. Things weren't well, really clean, and her daughter came in with that scruffy boyfriend of hers and the atmosphere was completely ruined. I don't think we need to risk that happening again.

DAUGHTER *(looking in her mother's direction, but her mother doesn't hear):* Perish the thought.

MOTHER: Yes, just leave it to me and I'll find somewhere else. . . . All right then, bye for now Sylvia.

(She hangs up the phone and starts writing on a piece of paper. She greets her daughter in a cooler voice than she was using on the phone and does not look up.)

MOTHER: Hello.

DAUGHTER: Hello.

MOTHER: How was school?

DAUGHTER: OK.

MOTHER: Will you have much homework this weekend?

DAUGHTER: No. I'm going to a party tomorrow night.

MOTHER *(looks up warily):* Are you asking me, or telling me.

DAUGHTER: Since you put it that was, I guess I'm telling you.

MOTHER: Well, I think I will tell you that you will not go.

DAUGHTER: Why not?

MOTHER: Well, to start with, you are only sixteen years old and it is still up to me where you go and don't go. Secondly, you haven't told me anything about this party or who's going. When is it?

DAUGHTER: Saturday night, tomorrow. I already said that.

MOTHER: Where?

DAUGHTER: Greg's place.

MOTHER: Isn't Greg that boy I heard about who was caught for drunken driving? On a motorcycle?

DAUGHTER: Yeah. That was a few months ago. He doesn't drink so much now.

MOTHER: Oh, I see. He doesn't drink *so much now.* And who else is going?

DAUGHTER: Just some kids from school. Don't hassle me Mom.

MOTHER: I cannot be happy about you associating with people I know nothing about.

DAUGHTER *(exasperated):* Mom, I've asked to have my friends over plenty of times. You always say no—you are too busy or something's getting fixed up or you just don't want people cluttering up your house and getting it messed up for your next meeting. Look, are you going to let me go to this party or not?

MOTHER: For all your talking, you still have told me nothing about who these people are. It doesn't sound like any of the young people from church will be there. I'm not about to let you go to a party where you will be in any kind of—danger.

DAUGHTER: Danger of what?

MOTHER: You know what I mean.

DAUGHTER: Sure I do. You're afraid I'll come home roaring drunk or get pregnant and that would embarrass you in front of the neighbors.

MOTHER *(very angry):* Don't you speak to me like that!

DAUGHTER: Well, you don't trust me, do you?

MOTHER: Yes I do. I know you wouldn't do anything to disgrace us.

DAUGHTER: Good, then I can go.

MOTHER *(looking away from her):* What would the people in church think if they knew you were allowed to go to non-Christian parties?

DAUGHTER: So you finally spit it out. That's what you've been thinking all along. You don't care what happens to me; you care about what the church people will think.

MOTHER: How can you say I don't care about you?

DAUGHTER: It always comes down to what people are going to think, doesn't it, Mom?

MOTHER: Why are you always trying to put me in a difficult situation?

DAUGHTER: Come off it. You can do that all by yourself.

MOTHER: All I've ever tried to do is raise you by the right principles and this is the thanks I get!

DAUGHTER: If the right principles mean this scene, *(Waves her arm around the room.)* I don't want them; stupid meetings all the time and hanging around with your snobby friends and eating coffee cake and gossiping about everyone who's not there. Very Christian.

MOTHER *(shouting):* That is a terrible thing to say! Stop insulting me, you selfish brat! *(After this outburst, shaken, she speaks more quietly.)* Your father and I have seen that you always had everything—everything you needed—and we have taught you the decent way to live and have exposed you to the best influences. How did you get to be so ungrateful?

DAUGHTER: Look, let's just cut this all short. If you won't let me go to the party then I'll have to stay home, but don't think you can change what I think about you!

(She walks out.)

MOTHER *(shouting):* Don't you walk away from me when I'm talking to you! Get back here!

Curtain.

Questions for Discussion

1. What values does the mother reveal in her phone conversation before the argument?

2. Where were the daughter's attitudes correct and where were they incorrect?

3. Where did each contribute to the argument?

4. What kind of impression has the mother's "Christianity" made on her daughter? Why?

5. How many other ways could the mother have responded to the daughter in this situation—especially when the daughter's accusations were true?

6. How should the daughter have responded to the mother in this situation?

7. Why is it so very difficult to maintain a Christian attitude around family members?

8. Since we are not perfect, those closest to us are going to see our worst sides. How can we use an unhappy family incident to grow closer to one another, and closer to God?

9. Dishonesty and role playing (hypocrisy) plays a big part in this skit and is the cause of a lot of family relationship problems. Discuss.

I Have Been Watching Too Much Television

If we expose ourselves to too much television we cannot help but suffer an erosion of values. We must also keep in mind that time spent watching TV is time taken away from other things. This skit shows how the life of a happy couple is destroyed when John becomes addicted to television. Only the most drastic measures can rescue him from TV's spell!

The setting is a living/dining area. At the left of the stage is a table with two chairs. In the center is a couch facing the audience and placed diagonally in front of the right side of the couch is a television (facing the couch, not the audience). To the right is a small table with a telephone, books, pad and pencil on it. The left entrance is a doorway to other parts of the house, the right entrance is the front door.

Throughout the play, a narrator will stand to the extreme left front of the stage and will do most of the talking while the action corresponds. Except when speech is attributed to characters in the script, all their conversation is mimed.

The action will take place as the narrator is speaking, except when he pauses to let the action and dialogue of the characters take over. Make sure that the drama and dialogue overlap so that there will not be any long pauses—either the narrator or the players should be speaking at all times.

Characters

Narrator—An eloquent, easy-to-listen-to person with a touch of a dry sense of humor.

John—A school teacher. He spends most of the skit in a moronic state, eyes glued to the TV.

Dorothy—His wife. The couple can be any age, from twenty through fifty.

Minister—Has the efficient, professional manner of a doctor.

(John and Dorothy are seated on the couch, miming conversation. They are looking at a large book together, pointing to pictures and talking animatedly.)

NARRATOR: Meet John and Dorothy, an outstanding couple. They have the kind of marriage and life-style that many would call ideal. John is a high school teacher, Dorothy works at home illustrating children's books. They are committed Christians and active in a nearby church; he as a deacon, she teaching teenage girls. They share a concern for poor people that led them to initiate an inner-city outreach program. They enjoy going to the theater and attend often with a group of friends. On weekends they go for visits to the country and Dorothy sketches the scenery while John takes photographs. Best of all, they simply take great pleasure in one another's company and never seem to run out of things to talk about. *(John and Dorothy close the book and exit left, still talking.)* It should be mentioned that there is a television in their home, but it has made very little intrusion into their lives. They watch the evening news before going to bed, and John enjoys the occasional football game; otherwise the television is hardly noticed.

(John enters right, looking tired and depressed. Dorothy enters from left, greets him, stops short of the couch and watches him, looking concerned.)

Until, one day, John came home from work tired and depressed from confrontations with delinquent sophomores and stodgy administrators.

(John throws himself on the couch. Dorothy remains where she is watching him.)

He didn't even have the energy to explain the situation to Dorothy, but threw himself numbly on the couch.

(John turns the television on.)

Then it happened. What motivated him is still unknown. Why he even thought of it still mystifies Dorothy, but the fact remains that at three o'clock on a weekday afternoon, John turned on the television . . . and watched a soap opera.

DOROTHY: John, why are you watching that? You have always despised and ridiculed soap operas.

JOHN: Dorothy, I need to unwind.

NARRATOR: Dorothy took refuge from the sounds of afternoon TV by remaining in the kitchen. (Dorothy exits left, leaving John watching TV.) John continued to watch television as the hours ticked by; after the soap operas, a sit-com rerun, then cartoons, then the news, followed by game shows, and still he watched—another sit-com, a movie, more news. Finally, after the late-night show, he turned off the television and went to bed. (John turns off TV and exits left.) After that fateful day, John's decline was swift. He became addicted to show after show. When he came home from school, he no longer talked to Dorothy about how his day had gone, or asked her about hers.

(John reenters from left, goes to TV and turns it on, sits on couch and watches it. Dorothy also enters from left with dishes and sets the table.)

Dorothy began to feel neglected, and was disturbed by the lack of communication between her and John.

DOROTHY: Dinner time, John. Please turn the TV off.

(John reluctantly turns it off, then goes to the table and begins gulping down his food.)

NARRATOR: John began rushing through his meals. In his haste to return to the television, he was seemingly unaware of what Dorothy had cooked.

JOHN: Dorothy, let's have dessert sitting on the couch; I don't want to miss the first game show.

(He rushes back to the TV. Dorothy throws up her hands in despair. Then she takes the dishes out left and reenters. She walks behind the couch to the telephone, dials, and after the narrator has finished, she begins talking. John remains watching television during the phone conversation, oblivious.)

NARRATOR: Dorothy became desperate, feeling powerless to turn the tide of her husband's decline. He became apathetic, never wanting to go out. He resented visits and phone calls because they cut into prime-time programs.

DOROTHY (on the phone): Mother, I just don't know what to do about John. It's getting to the stage where I'm afraid to have people over—he's so unresponsive. He's just not the man I married! (Pause.) Yes, he's lazy, he doesn't enjoy his work anymore, he never discusses my work with me—he doesn't seem to know I'm here! And worst of all—he's even lost interest in the Lord's work! He resents anything he's asked to do for the church, and he even let me go to the last two outreach meetings alone! He said he was too tired, but I know it's because the meetings are on Thursday night when one of his favorite programs is on. I'm just beside myself. (Pause.) Yes, OK, I will come over tomorrow. Bye. (She hangs up and addresses John.) Come on John, it's time to go to bed. (She turns off the TV, takes him by the arm and they exit left.)

(John reenters from left and turns television on then sits on *the couch. His face has a stupid look and his eyes look glazed over.)*

NARRATOR: As the situation worsened, John's communication was reduced to monosyllables. He couldn't concentrate on correcting his students' work for more than fifteen minutes at a time, after which he found himself longing for a commercial break. When Dorothy caught him sounding out the word "proceed" on a traffic sign, she began to fear he was losing his ability to read—a serious handicap for an English teacher. *(Dorothy enters from left and stands near the couch.)* Dorothy tried every device she could in an effort to lure him away from the TV. She suggested outings.

DOROTHY: John, let's go out for dinner tonight.

JOHN: Sure, we'll go to that pizza joint down the street that has the large video screen. We can watch the movie. Ten minutes till it starts—we'd better grab our coats and go. *(He grabs her arm and they exit left.)*

NARRATOR: Poor Dorothy even tried to camouflage the television set.

(Dorothy enters left, tiptoeing and peering anxiously behind her. She is holding a tablecloth and a potted plant. She goes to the TV, puts the tablecloth over it and places the plant on top. She sits on the couch and folds her hands as John enters from left. He looks immediately at the TV.)

JOHN: Hey Dorothy, why did you put a tablecloth and a plant on the TV? *(Dorothy shrugs. John removes the plant and cloth and places them out of the way near the couch.)* You know, you're acting a little strange lately. *(He turns on the TV, sits down and watches it.)*

NARRATOR: Dorothy knew she would have to call for outside help when John refused to go to church on Sunday morning, offering the excuse that the televised church services needed viewer support so the networks would not replace them with sports broadcasts. Dorothy summoned the minister.

(A knock is heard at the front door and Dorothy goes and lets in the minister who is carrying a bag similar to a doctor's bag. He walks directly over to John, who is oblivious of his presence.)

DOROTHY: His condition is worsening every day. He seems to be losing his mind! It's as though he's sleepwalking, and the only time he ever speaks is to tell me what show he wants to watch.

MINISTER: Hmm. *(Pulling up John's eyelids to examine his eyes.)* How long since you first noticed him watching too much?

DOROTHY: It happened all of a sudden, about a month ago.

MINISTER: How long have his eyes been glazed over? *(Waves his hand in front of John, but he doesn't blink.)*

DOROTHY: About two weeks.

MINISTER: Well, he's in the advanced stages.

DOROTHY *(alarmed):* Advanced stages of what?

MINISTER: Televisionism. It's ravaging our congregations. Strikes the most unlikely people. Some of them have gone past the stage of recovery.

DOROTHY: Oh no!

MINISTER *(goes to Dorothy and pats her shoulder):* It's OK Dorothy. You called me in time. There's still hope for him. But we'll have to work fast.

DOROTHY: What do we do?

MINISTER: There's only one thing to do—we've got to get it out of his system fast. We've got to cut him right off—cold turkey.

DOROTHY: What will it do to him?

MINISTER: Well, he could go through a violent withdrawal. I know this is traumatic for you, Dorothy, but I think it would be safest if we tied him down. Then we're going to have to go through the deprogramming procedure—expose him to the elements of real life that he valued before the televisionism set in. It could take hours. Do you think you can go through with it, Dorothy?

DOROTHY: I'm ready.

NARRATOR: The most violent part of the whole procedure was to remove the TV from John's gaze.

(The minister gets a rope out of his black bag and they tie John to the couch. He remains oblivious. After tying him, the minister unplugs the television. John lets out a wail of despair. The minister carries the television out the door while Dorothy goes to John and comforts him.

JOHN: Dorothy, where is he taking my TV?

DOROTHY: It's OK John. Everything's going to be all right. I know it seems cruel but we have to take the TV away from you. You are addicted and it's ruining your life.

JOHN (wails): No! Give me back my TV. There's something I've got to see!

MINISTER (reenters from right and removes a book from his bag): John, try to listen to me. I want to help you. I'm going to read to you for a while and I want you to concentrate on what I am saying.

(Minister reads from Bible, John writhes in discomfort. Dorothy and him begin having an exaggerated conversation in front of John, and he continues to toss his head from side to side and moan.)

NARRATOR: First the minister read stirring passages of the Bible to John. Then he instructed Dorothy to discuss with him various aspects of the church's activities in an effort to remind John of his interests and reacquaint him with the procedure of conversation. After an hour, John was still oblivious to what they were saying, so Dorothy tried showing him several of the children's books she had illustrated.

(Minister and Dorothy show signs of fatigue. Minister loosens his tie. Dorothy goes to table and gets childrens books. Begins showing pictures to John.)

(John calms down a little and half-listens to Dorothy.)

NARRATOR: This visually-oriented activity seemed to calm John somewhat, and he was slightly more attentive. When, however, John glanced at his watch and realized he was missing the late movie—a Fred Astaire and Ginger Rogers feature, he groaned and his condition seemed to deteriorate. *(John glances at his watch, groans and resumes writhing around. Minister kneels near John and speaks to him with intensity.)* The minister then addressed John directly, reminding him of his responsibilities in life and describing the many things he had taken pleasure in only a month ago.

(Minister gets up, runs his hand through his hair and sways slightly. Dorothy, also looking extremely tired, picks up a piece of paper from the table and begins reading from it.)

The night passed. Dorothy and the minister became exhausted. As dawn approached, they were nearly ready to give up. Dorothy was reading him his English syllabus for the rest of the year in an effort to arouse his spirit of dedication to teaching, when suddenly, it happened. *(John blinks and opens his eyes wide, cocks his head.)* A look of intelligence returned to his eyes, his head cocked attentively as though he recalled some long forgotten dream. He sat up, as far as the ropes would allow, and spoke.

JOHN *(as he straightens his posture)*: Pencil! Paper!

DOROTHY *(excited)*: He's speaking to us!

MINISTER: Quick—get them!

(Dorothy runs to the phone table and returns with pad and pencil, which she hands to John. John writes slowly and deliberately. He hands the pad back to Dorothy.)

DOROTHY: It says, "I think I have been watching too much television!"

MINISTER: Aha! Admission of the condition! The first step to recovery!

(John drops his head back on the couch and falls asleep. Dorothy and the pastor shake hands and both untie John.)

NARRATOR: Indeed it was the first step to a rapid and complete recovery. John fell into an exhausted sleep, the Salvation Army took the television away, and in its absence, John and Dorothy resumed their former rich, productive and happy life.

(John stands and all bow.)

Questions for Discussion

1. How much time do you spend watching television each week?

2. What programs can you just not miss? Why?

3. If your TV were taken away, what would you do with the time you normally spend watching it?

4. What are some of the positive aspects of having a television?

5. Give examples of programs that glamorize anti-Christian behavior such as violence, sexual and ethical immorality, selfishness, and disrespect for authority (including God). Is there any harm in watching programs like these?

6. What makes watching television so addictive? What can we do to keep TV watching under control in our homes?

7. Many television programs and most commercials promote a life-style of luxury and self-centeredness. What effect can this have on a person who is struggling with the Christian concepts of generosity and self-sacrifice?

8. Do we (or our children) get appropriate role models or appropriate goals for our life from watching television?

Inner Turmoil

Living as a Christian does not mean just going through a series of "spiritual activities," it means surrendering the whole being to God. We can be doing all the right things in the eyes of other people but not be surrendered to the Lord.

This skit examines one such person. It consists of a dialogue between the person's self and his or her conscience—the struggle of human nature. One actor (or actress) represents the self and one the conscience. They should be similar in appearance and dressed the same. The conscience will sit on a stool placed slightly to the right of the stage (the only prop required) and the self will pace around on the left side of the stage during the dialogue. You may want to explain to the audience that the play involves dialogue between one person's self and conscience or let one person wear a sign that says "self," and the other wear a sign that says "conscience." Otherwise the conscience could be mistaken for another person.

Characters

Self—a busy, apparently "successful" Christian who displays confidence but deep down is disturbed and unhappy—a condition that reveals itself by the end of the skit.

Conscience—speaks with a firm and persuasive voice, but is not loud or preachy.

(Self enters from left at the same time conscience enters from right.)

SELF: All things, considered, I'm really doing pretty well as a Christian. I mean, I've got the daily Bible reading and prayer part all together, I'm going to the morning and evening services and I'm doing so much Christian work I never even have time to watch television!

CONSCIENCE: Come off it. Don't be so shallow. You know there's more to it than that.

SELF: What do you mean?

CONSCIENCE: Remember the part about dying to yourself?

SELF: I don't know what you're getting at.

CONSCIENCE: Stop being so stubborn. What's the point of playing games with me?

SELF: Look, I'm busy. I certainly haven't got time to unravel the mysterious messages of a distant conscience.

CONSCIENCE: I seem distant only because you are not used to listening to me. You will never get anywhere until you listen to me. You can't ignore me and grow closer to God no matter what else you do.

SELF: Look! I've got nothing to be ashamed of. Just the other day one of the youth-group leaders told me I was the most dependable person in the group. And the most hard-working.

CONSCIENCE: I'm not talking about your external behavior.

SELF: Do you know how much of the Bible I've committed to memory?

CONSCIENCE: How much have you committed to heart?

(Self is growing exasperated and talking louder.)

SELF: I witness *every* day. Not many people do that.

CONSCIENCE: Lots of people witness every day—from many different motives.

SELF: Don't hassle me about motives. I get the job done.

CONSCIENCE: What's the job? Do you ever give any thought to what the job is, or do you, perhaps, go through the acceptable, commendable motions?

SELF: Why are you being so hard on me?

CONSCIENCE: Because it's my job to make sure you never feel comfortable with pride or ignorance or selfishness, or any of the other things that keep you from knowing God.

SELF *(surrendering reluctantly):* All right then, what are you trying to tell me? And try to make it clear for once.

CONSCIENCE: Despite all your righteous activity and the praises of other people, you don't feel at peace, do you?

SELF: Always asking questions aren't you?

CONSCIENCE: Answer.

SELF *(pauses):* OK—no. I don't feel peaceful. . . . I admit, I feel as though something is missing. Some other Christians have something I don't. *(Being honest now.)* I keep trying to get hold of it, I keep figuring maybe I can earn it or something, even though I'm not even sure what "it" is.

CONSCIENCE: Tell yourself the verse about dying to self.

SELF: Sure, I know that one. *(Rattles it off.)* "It is no longer I who lives but Christ who lives in me and the life I now live in the body I live by faith in the Son of God who loved me and gave Himself for me." Yeah . . . so?

CONSCIENCE: Answer this—what did you think about when you woke up this morning?

SELF: Oh man, I don't remember.

CONSCIENCE: Think.

SELF: Just what I was going to do today. *(Speaking slowly, thinking out loud.)* How I would study, then go to volleyball practice then go to the concert tonight. There's nothing wrong with any of that—it's a Christian concert.

'

CONSCIENCE: Why do you study?

SELF *(impatient):* What do you mean, why do I study?

CONSCIENCE: What is your motive for studying?

SELF: To do well. To be successful.

CONSCIENCE: What is your motive for practicing?

SELF: To do well. To be good at it.

CONSCIENCE: What is your motive for going to the concert?

SELF: To see Jeff Thompson, because I found out he's going too. *(Use a girl's name if your players are boys.)*

CONSCIENCE: Is your love for God tied up at all in any of those motives?

SELF *(exasperated):* Oh, come on. There is absolutely nothing wrong with any of those things, or my motives!

CONSCIENCE: Your life must not consist of simply avoiding wrong things. I am trying to get you to realize *who* you are living for!

SELF *(quietly):* Oh.

CONSCIENCE: Tell me how you go about making decisions.

SELF *(finally catching on, speaking more quietly):* I guess I pretty much do what I want . . . or maybe what will make me look good to other people.

CONSCIENCE: Who gets the glory for your achievements?

SELF *(looks down):* Me.

CONSCIENCE *(pauses):* Do you love God?

SELF *(looks at Conscience for about five seconds before speaking, obviously disturbed):* Not as much as I'd like to—not as much as I pretend to.

CONSCIENCE: Then you are not very different from what you were before you heard of Christ.

SELF *(humbly):* I don't understand what you are asking of me.

CONSCIENCE: You know the teaching about dying. You have His example. You know the teaching about loving. You have His example.

SELF: I don't know how to—die to myself—or to love, really.

CONSCIENCE: God does not tell you to do impossible things. He always gives the power along with the command.

SELF: What you are saying is that I have to start all over again, so to speak. All this goodness I have built up for myself in doing good things doesn't count, does it?

CONSCIENCE: Nope.

SELF: Well . . . I haven't been very happy. God has seemed far away even though I'm always talking about Him. So I guess I have to take some time out and just concentrate on God. Is that right?

CONSCIENCE: Sounds like a good idea.

SELF: And just pray about what I should be doing, and then do things for Him and not for me?

CONSCIENCE: And let His Spirit help you.

SELF: Yeah. That's how I want to learn to live.

CONSCIENCE *(smiles):* That's a good choice.

SELF *(looking at audience):* I'm glad I decided that.

(Self follows Conscience off stage right.)

Questions for Discussion

1. How was the person in this skit deceiving himself/herself?

2. What is the difference between just being involved in Christian activities and being a committed follower of Jesus?

3. How do you feel when someone tells you that being a Christian means dying to self?

4. What does it really mean to die to self?

5. How can we make sure that our conscience is in keeping with the Word of God?

6. How do you react when your conscience is pricking you about something?

7. 1 Timothy 4 relates that "some shall depart from the faith . . . , having their conscience seared. . . ." How does a conscience become seared? Can an individual sear his or her own conscience? How can we guard against that?

8. Is the reverse true? Can we train our own consciences? Can our consciences be trained incorrectly? Can we receive help in training our own conscience—give help in training others?

9. The Bible does not have much to say regarding the conscience, but has a great deal to say regarding obedience to God. In light of that, what do you think of the saying, "let your conscience be your guide"?

Out of Service

This is a series of role plays—six people who have an attitude that is preventing them from serving the Lord effectively. You might choose to stop after each role play and discuss what in the person's attitude is hampering him.

Characters

1. **A legalistic person.** All motives for Christian conduct are linked to pride. His manner is arrogant.

2. **A negative, rationalizing person.** She uses problems as an excuse for not submitting to God's will. She does not realize that God has the power to overcome problems.

3. **An unrealistic person.** Interested in the rewards and fun of Christian living, but with little commitment to the Lord. He has a superficial glib manner.

4. **An underconfident person.** She has such low self esteem she does not believe that God wants to use her. Her manner is shy and self-effacing.

5. **A loner** who wants to live in a way that gives him pleasure under the guise of Christian liberty. Has no conception of the responsibilities, privileges and demands of being part of the church.

6. **An uptight person.** She has not learned to rest in faith in God, but is racing around in frantic efforts to do the right thing, wearing herself out in the process.

1. The Legalistic Christian

(Legalistic Christian enters, carrying a large black Bible, addresses audience.)

I am a very spiritual Christian. That is obvious to anyone who has had a chance to observe my blameless life-style.

I accepted Christ at the age of seven, so for as long as I can remember I have been a member of the Kingdom of God. For this reason I have very little trouble with ungodly attitudes— the Lord has always had His hand upon me.

I am thoroughly grounded in the Word of God. Since the age of five I have had increasingly long devotions that have grown to an average duration of two-and-a-half hours. I have memorized a hundred and thirty-two Scripture passages and read the Bible twenty times.

When I pray, I kneel on a hard wooden floor by my bed, where my knees are beginning to wear two indentations in the floor, as have the knees of spiritual giants before me.

The cross I have to bear in my life, not surprisingly, is the spiritual immaturity of all other members of my church. Their lack of discipline, commitment, and zeal is a constant source of pain to me. I have taken it upon myself to bring them out of their babyhood by leading them in a course of rigorous Bible study. *(Pauses.)* Attendance to date has been . . . rather low, but I am praying that more will become clear sighted about their failings and come to me for help.

I think my greatest attribute lies in the fact that I have brought all areas of my life into total subjection to Christ. There is not one indulgent activity or unfruitful pursuit in my entire timetable. Now I admit that not all people have the same potential, and some of you may be unable to reach my standard, but I would like to encourage you to take note of the qualities you have seen in me, and strive to attain them for yourselves. *(He exits.)*

2. The Rationalizing Christian

(Rationalizing Christian enters, with a slumped posture and a depressed expression. Addresses audience.)

Well, spiritual growth may be possible for some people but they don't have the problems I've got. You know, the thought of doing all those good things for God is great, but I'm so loaded down with worries I don't have the time or the energy.

I mean, what chance did I ever have in life? My father died when I was a kid, and as soon as I turned sixteen I had to start work to support my mother and five brothers and sisters. I never had what other people had, and now my mother is old and has arthritis and I can hardly ever leave the house because she needs me to take care of her all the time. All this talk about church involvement and helping needy people and going to the mission field is just out of the question for me.

I'm not a healthy person either. I get headaches and boils, and suffer from allergies and bronchitis, not to mention middle-ear infections. My doctor agrees with me that I am very restricted in all my activities.

And you know, what really annoys me is when people talk about how a Christian is supposed to spend time with God—praying and reading the Bible. That's just not always practical. My life is full of distractions, and reading small print gives me a tension headache, and if you lived around here you'd give up anything that demanded peace and quiet. We've got neighbors next door with ten kids and neighbors on the other side who keeps chickens and a guy across the street who plays drums. You might as well try to pray in downtown Manhattan during rush hour.

So as you can see, this whole business of being a servant of God is great in theory but I'm afraid in my circumstances it just isn't possible. *(She exits.)*

3. The Unrealistic Christian

(Unrealistic Christian enters, walking briskly and smiling. Waves to the congregation and addresses it.)

Hello congregation! And how are you all? I trust you are all going strong in the Lord!

You know, I am happy to be here with you all today and I hope you are happy too. I think Christians should be happy all the time! I mean we are so fortunate. There are so many advantages to being a Christian! I accepted Jesus into my life last year, and since then everything has gone so well for me! Just let me give you an example.

I'm a door-to-door salesperson, and now that I'm a Christian I never knock on anyone's door before I repeat to myself five times, "I can do all things through Christ who strengthens me," and do you know—I sell three times more than I ever sold before! What a blessing.

And doing God's work is so much fun! I teach and help lead the youth group, and you know, the kids just love it. We play games and go to movies and have parties—I haven't made the mistake some youth leaders make of emphasizing heavy spiritual things too much—you don't want to scare the kids off!

I just can't understand these people who say that being a servant of God is such a hard life. I don't think the Bible says anything about that. . . . Actually I'm not sure about that because I can't say that I get enough time to read much of the Bible, but it sure never comes out in the choruses we sing!

I just can't figure out why everyone doesn't become a Christian—we can let God handle all our problems and just be happy! *(He exits.)*

4. The Underconfident Christian

(Underconfident Christian enters, wearing an apron and addresses the audience with her hands folded in front of her.)

Hi. I'm just a housewife. All this talk about being the Lord's servant makes me feel pretty useless. All I know how to do is clean the house and wash diapers and feed babies. I don't have any abilities, really.

I guess I have always been a pretty shy person. Like in Bible studies and discussion groups—everyone else seems to have something helpful to say but I just sit there, feeling dumb. Sometimes I know the answers—I read my Bible a lot—but I can't ever get the words to come out right, so I feel even dumber when I try to talk than if I just sit there and don't say anything. So I avoid those kind of gatherings now.

Our minister talks a lot about using our spiritual gifts—being evangelists and that sort of thing—but I'm sure I could never talk to people about the Lord. It's not that I don't want to—I love God and I know everyone needs to hear about Jesus—but I know that people wouldn't pay any attention to what I have to say.

I do feel left out of things. So many other Christians are doing things like teaching and preaching and organizing socials. I feel useless; I wish I had a different personality.

I know it's not God's fault that I'm the way I am. I'm afraid I might have done something to displease Him so He can't use me—I don't know.

(She exits.)

5. The Lone-Ranger Christian

(Lone-Ranger Christian enters, and addresses the audience standing in a relaxed position, in a confident, casual manner.)

I suppose you could say I'm a kind of an independent Christian —a loner. That's mainly because you usually meet other Christians in churches, and I can't stand churches. Most of them are so culturally backward, so out of touch with society. And so many Christians are bound up with irrelevant rules— don't do this and don't do that.

When I think of a typical church-goer, I think of someone who's a little on the dull side; hung up, self-righteous. Patting themselves on the back because they don't go to R-rated movies or say naughty words.

Well, I think they are all completely off the track. If I read things correctly, Jesus came to set us free—to give us abundant life. So, I live abundantly *(smiles).*

I was talking to a Christian the other day who said I shouldn't spend so much of my time at parties and going to bars; that I was cutting myself off from "fellowship." I told her that if she thought I needed "fellowship" so badly she could meet me downtown for a drink next Friday night. She said she didn't drink and pretty soon she left—sort of ticked off at me but trying not to show it, like she was trying to do her good deed for the day but I was beyond all hope.

And that's what I am getting at—she was so judgmental and unaccepting. Who needs fellowship with a bunch of hung-up people? They don't want me in their churches and I certainly don't need them. I'll just be a Christian in my own way. *(He exits.)*

6. The Uptight Christian

(Uptight Christian enters, with anxious facial expression, hurried walk, addresses audience in an agitated voice, with nervous gestures.)

Boy, I just can't believe how fast the time gets away from me. I mean, there's too much to be done. Sometimes I wonder how we're supposed to do everything we're called to do; us Christians, I mean. I really worry about that.

Whatever I'm doing, I always feel like I should be doing something else—there's this constant conflict, you know? If I'm really concentrating on my job at work, I feel guilty that I'm not taking time out to get to know the other people at work and showing them that I care about them, but if I'm talking instead of doing my job, I feel like I'm cheating the company and that's a bad witness.

And if I stay home after work and spend time with my family, I feel as though I should be out doing the Lord's work, visitation or church committee work or something. But whenever I get involved in something that takes me away from home I feel guilty for neglecting my family! And if I don't watch TV and keep up with the news in the papers, I feel like I'm losing touch with the world, but if I do, I feel I'm being corrupted by the world. You just can't win.

I am literally exhausted trying to be everything I'm supposed to be, and I still feel like I'm failing miserably. I can't even sleep at night. I worry about people's problems and I think of the things ahead of me in my schedule. I try to pray about what worries me, but I get hung up because I know I don't have enough faith to really believe God will fix everything and I start to worry about how I must be making God angry because I don't have enough faith, so then I can't concentrate on praying anymore.

Sometimes I wonder whether I really *am* a Christian at all—surely I wouldn't be this miserable and confused if I really were saved. *(She exits, rubbing her forehead.)*

Questions for Discussion

1. Discuss each of the personalities *(either after each role play or after they are all finished)* and define what attitudes prevented them from being effective servants.

2. What is involved in the concept of serving the Lord? Does it refer only to "Christian" activities?

3. How would you feel if a legalistic Christian described his Christian life to you? What was positive and what was negative about this person's attitude and habits?

4. In light of verses like James 1:2, 3 and 2 Corinthians 11:24-33, is it valid to attribute lack of spiritual growth to physical problems (as the rationalizing Christian did)?

5. Should Christians be happy all the time? Do non-Christians expect this? Does God?

6. What advice would you give the underconfident Christian?

7. Do you think the Lone-Ranger Christian's description of the average churchgoer is accurate?

8. How can an uptight Christian find joy? What very real problems may cause a Christian to be uptight? How can we deal with this tendency to take on the problems of the world?

Why Jog When You Can Roller Skate?

This skit compares a Christian who is relying on his own strength to do right with one who understands that God wishes to supply the power we need for living. The stage needs a surface suitable for roller skating, but there are no other prop or scenery requirements.

Characters

Self Effort—bearing his name on his T-shirt, is in a state of perpetual motion, trying and trying to improve his track record. (Get a fit actor.)

Grace—also bearing his name on his T-shirt, is finding the going much easier. (Get an actor who can roller skate well.)

(Self Effort jogs on stage, checking his speed with a stop-watch. When he speaks, he jogs on the spot. He is energetic to start with, and addressed God as he jogs.)

SELF EFFORT: How'm I doing, Master Coach? Pretty good, eh? This is the most ground I've covered by noon so far. *(Looks at watch.)* Yep, I'm doing more all the time! Better and better!

(Jogs for a while in silence, then does some vigorous exercises. He is beginning to breathe heavily.)

Wow, I have to admit it's tough going, training with You, but I have the satisfaction of knowing You're the best Coach around!

(More jogging, he's getting tired and slows down.)

Oh boy. I guess I have a long way to go before I get up to Your standard!

(More jogging and his face is showing the strain. He starts staggering.)

Oh my! I don't know how much longer I can keep this up.

(Grace enters on roller skates, looking happy and composed. He swirls to a stop as he passes Self Effort and looks concerned at his obvious exhaustion.)

GRACE: Hi! Hey, what on earth are you doing—you look exhausted!

(Self Effort finally stops. Panting, he points to Grace's roller skates.)

SELF EFFORT: Where did you get those roller skates?

GRACE: He gave them to me of course. The Master.

SELF EFFORT: He gave them to you? What for?

GRACE *(shrugs)*: To make it easier to get around—so I can get things done—and, to enjoy myself!

SELF EFFORT: You mean the Coach just *gave* them to you?

GRACE: Sure, everyone can have them. You know that don't you?

SELF EFFORT *(feeling left out)*: No! Why didn't anyone tell me about them?

GRACE: Well, you get them the first time you go before the Master.

SELF EFFORT *(looks ashamed)*: Oh.

GRACE: Hey, don't tell me you haven't been going to see Him —spending some time with Him.

SELF EFFORT *(defensive)*: Well, I've been busy. *(With pride.)* I've been building myself up. I want to come up to the Coach's level.

GRACE *(astonished)*: Is that why you've been burning yourself out? You're on a self-effort trip? Man, you can't come up to His level! None of us can. Ten minutes with Him and you'd realize that. *(Shaking his head.)* No way.

SELF EFFORT: Well, what are we supposed to do then?

GRACE: You have totally misunderstood the whole relationship between us and the Master.

SELF EFFORT: What do you mean?

GRACE: We can't be winners on our own steam. That's why we need Him. And He *does* want to spend His time with losers—not that we're supposed to be down on ourselves or not try—but we have to realize that we aren't complete without Him. *(Pause.)* He's waiting to help you. I mean it. You've got to go see Him—get some roller skates to start with, then let Him change some of your attitudes. OK?

SELF EFFORT: Yeah, OK, I'll do that. Thanks for the advice.

GRACE: Hey, that's all right. Just take it easy. *(He continues skating, exiting on the opposite side of where he entered. As he leaves he shakes his head, and says.)* Boy, the way some people live!

SELF EFFORT *(to himself):* I'd better go see Him right away. . . . Roller skates, eh? What a relief.

(He walks off, using the same exit as Grace.)

Questions for Discussion

1. Why did Self Effort miss out on the roller skates? What is the parallel for Christians?

2. In what ways do we exhibit self effort in our lives as Christians?

3. Why do we go back to living within our own limitations after the Holy Spirit has empowered us?

4. If we emphasize grace, will that give us license to sin? See Romans 6:1-4.

5. What can we do to ensure that we continue in God's grace?

6. What forces or influences in our society drive us toward self effort? How do these teachings conflict with Biblical teachings of reliance on God?

7. How do pride and humility play parts in the conflict between grace and self effort?

George, the Soul-Winning Dentist

The Christian with the best intentions can do a lot of damage in his attempts to witness by being insensitive. One of the most disturbing aspects of some evangelism programs is the failure to really care for people as individuals rather than as statistics. When this impersonal attitude is sensed in a Christian, he loses credibility.

This is George's problem, and in this skit he foists the gospel on a captive patient.

A reclining deck chair can substitute for the dentist's chair that will be needed for this office setting. Other props needed will be a tooth chart, a huge poster on the back wall, reading, "I fix your teeth but Jesus fixes your soul" and a tray for the nurse. All the other equipment can be left to the imagination, though the actor may go to elaborate measures to gather dental equipment—even to the point of using the sound of a drill (off-stage)!

The chair should be placed diagonally near the center of the stage, so the faces of both the patient and the doctor can be seen.

Characters

George—an energetic, forceful, talkative dentist, intent on "winning souls."

Greg—an unsuspecting patient. He becomes increasingly afraid of George as the skit progresses, but rarely gets a chance to speak because his mouth will be full of cotton balls and instruments.

Nurse—Stands near George to hand him instruments but never speaks. She remains indifferent throughout the skit.

(George is washing his hands at an imaginary sink to the left of the stage. When he finishes, he bounds over to the other side of the stage, near the right entrance, and calls.)

GEORGE: Next please! *(Rubs hands in anticipation.)*

(Greg enters and stands in doorway, looking apprehensive.)

GEORGE: Hi there. You must be Greg.

GREG: Uh, yeah.

GEORGE: Well, I'm glad to meet you, Greg. This is the first time you've been here, isn't it?

GREG: Yes.

GEORGE *(rubs his hands together again and looks at audience):* Aha! Raw material! *(Greg's eyes widen and he glances back at the doorway.)*

GEORGE *(takes him by the shoulders and escorts him to the chair):* Now you just sit here and relax, Son. You're going to benefit more from this visit than you anticipated! Now what's the trouble, or is this just a checkup?

(Nurse enters and takes up her position a few feet from George.)

GREG: I have a bad toothache in this back molar on the bottom. *(Pointing inside his mouth.)* I guess I've got a cavity.

GEORGE *(grabbing mirror and tongue depressor from tray):* Sure thing! We'll have you fixed up before you can say ouch! *(Begins probing his tooth.)* Now tell me, Boy, are you saved? *(Adjusts imaginary overhead light.)*

GREG: What did you say, Sir?

GEORGE: I said, are you saved, washed in the blood?

GREG: Well, I don't really know what that. . . .

GEORGE: Open up. *(Begins inspecting tooth again.)* Thought not. I come across it all the time. Young people who think they can make it without the Savior. Or worse, not even knowing about Him. What are their parents thinking of? Suction.

(Nurse hands him scraping tool and tube, which he places in the patient's mouth. Greg will have to keep his mouth slightly open for the rest of the skit.)

GEORGE: Tell me Son, do you know the Gospel?

(Greg makes a few gargling sounds.)

GEORGE: Well, I'm not going to let another day go by without you getting to hear it! *(Continues scraping tooth.)* It's like this. Men are all miserable sinners, everyone of us, you included. But for the wonderful grace of God we would all be justly condemned to everlasting Hell. But God in His wonderful mercy has given us the chance for redemption

78

through the sacrifice of the Lamb at Calvary. Yup, Son, and all we have to do is accept Jesus as our Savior, and we will become heirs to everlasting glory. Could I make it any clearer than that?

(Greg gargles again in an attempt to answer.)

GEORGE *(to nurse):* Get a shot ready, Clara. I'm going to drill. *(Nurse picks up the imaginary needle and pretends to eject the first bit of liquid.)* Yes, Boy, you sure have a big black cavity in there, but it's not as black as your heart is in the eyes of a righteous and holy God. *(His voice is growing louder, like a preacher preaching his main point.)* Needle Clara. *(Nurse hands him the needle. Greg's eyes widen in horror)* Am I starting to get through to you, Son?

(Greg nods vigorously, eyes fixed on the needle.)

GEORGE *(smiles):* Good. Now this shouldn't hurt much at all. *(Injects in the area where Greg pointed to the cavity. Starts to stuff cotton in his mouth.)* Yes, I can't help drawing a parallel between my work and the ministry of the Holy Ghost. I relieve the pain and stop the decay—He relieves an aching heart and purifies the soul.

(Begins to drill and sings "Amazing Grace" as Greg grips the chair arms and winces. When he finishes, he puts drill on tray and picks up a filling instrument.)

GEORGE: Hurt a little too much for you, did it? *(Greg makes a muffled noise.)* Well, the pain is worth the prize and how much more in the spiritual realm! *(Fills the tooth.)*

GEORGE: Now, Boy, I want you to remember some verses from the Holy Word of God. First, Romans 3 verse 23: "For all have sinned, and come short of the glory of God." Got that?

(Greg shrugs.)

GEORGE: *(Louder and more threatening):* Got that?

(Greg nods, convinced that the doctor is a lunatic.)

GEORGE: Then get the next one. Romans 6 verse 23—"For the wages of sin is death; but the gift of God is eternal life through Jesus Christ our Lord." Got that?

(Greg nods.)

And John 1:12—"But as many as received him, to them gave he power to become the sons of God." Make sense to you, Boy?

(Greg nods enthusiastically.)

GEORGE: Good. Then there is nothing stopping you from being born again. *(Pulls the cotton out of his mouth.)* Sit up and rinse now. *(Nurse moves around to the other side of chair, hands him imaginary cup of water and holds imaginary bowl for him to spit into. Greg rinses, then moves to get up. George pushed him back into the chair.)* We're not quite finished, Boy! *(Greg eyes him warily.)* Now I'm going to say a prayer on your behalf and you are going to pray along in your heart of hearts, right? *(Nurse exits.)*

GREG *(with a resigned attitude):* OK.

GEORGE *(closes his eyes and looks heavenward):* Gracious Heavenly Father, hear the prayer of your faithful servant on behalf of this miserable sinner. This lost sheep now desires to come into Your fold. He wants to repent of all his evil and pledge everlasting devotion to You. Please accept him into your fold, Dear Father. Amen. *(Smiles a satisfied smile.)* Well, Boy, you're on your way to a new way of living now! Get up! What are you sitting there looking stupid for? It's time to get out and preach the Word!

GREG *(scrambling up):* Uh, thanks. . . .

GEORGE: Go on, go on! I know you can't express the depth of your gratitude, but it's all in a day's work for me!

(He walks Greg to the door. Greg, with one last bewildered stare, leaves. George looks after him with arms folded and a smile of satisfaction.)

There he goes. The light of glory in his eyes. Yup, they don't call me "George, the Soul-Winning Dentist" for nothing!

Questions for Discussion

1. What was wrong with George's attitude toward Greg? How was he viewing Greg?

2. How would you feel if someone came up to you and asked, "Are you saved?"

3. What mistakes can someone who is eager to witness make in dealing with people?

4. Can you remember conversations in which people either witnessed to you before you were a Christian, or counseled you in growth as a Christian? What qualities in them did or did not appeal to you?

5. What impressions of Christianity would George give to a non-Christian person?

6. What are some appropriate ways to approach people?

7. There are some people who are this overt in their witnessing, but more often, what is the problem?

8. Is it possible to let the fear of seeming obnoxious keep us from saying anything at all? Discuss.

A Warm Welcome to Our Visitors

Visitors to our church too often receive anything but a warm welcome. This may be because we are too absorbed in our own affairs and lack a vision for outreach, or we may simply be unaware of who the visitors are.

The purpose of this skit is to wake people up to the needs of visitors. We must discern their situations to make them feel welcome and relaxed. First impressions are vital!

The setting is outside a church. You may want to make the entrance to the stage look like the outside of a church door. The main characters, Steve and Margery, are standing outside in vain hopes that someone will stop and talk to them. The church members will enter as though they are leaving the church building, walk past them and exit on the other side of the stage. The skit's humor and message rests on the fact that the church people are too absorbed to notice the newcomers. Success of the skit relies heavily on the character of Steve and he provides the climax in his desperation to get someone's attention.

Characters

Steve—very emotional man. Makes wild gestures, has intense expressions, and a dramatic way of speaking.

Margery—his more sedate wife.

Church members—Two middle-aged men, a man and a wife, two women, an old man, three more groups of people of at least three to a group, and the minister and his wife.

(Margery and Steve enter from church and stop center stage.)

STEVE: Now that was a terrific sermon. At least one church in this area has a good preacher.

MARGERY: He was the first one who has even mentioned outreach. All the other churches were like social clubs. I felt like it would have been easier to get accepted into a country club than one of those churches.

STEVE: Yeah. Now if the people here are friendly, I think we may have found a congregation worth considering.

(Two men enter, talking excitedly. They do not see Margery and Steve. Steve smiles and waits for them to see him, but they keep walking.)

MAN 1: Boy, that guy sure gets you stirred up, doesn't he, Jim? He makes me want to hit the streets and witness to all those unsaved folks before another day goes by!

MAN 2: You said it Fred. He made me want to reach out and hug everyone!

MARGERY *(looking after them)*: I didn't expect a hug. A handshake would have sufficed.

MAN 1 *(pausing before exiting)*: You know, that sermon gave me a real burden for some of the guys in my golf club.

MAN 2 *(as they exit)*: Yeah? You know, speaking of golf . . .

(They exit.)

STEVE: Well, they didn't see us. We have to give people a chance. Here comes a couple about our age.

(Couple enters, walking slowly.)

WIFE: The preacher was right, you know. Our church isn't

anything like those New Testament churches. But what should we do about it?

HUSBAND: Well, honey, I don't think we should feel guilty—I don't think we're doing anything wrong. It's just that in this day and age things are more complicated. You need more educated church leaders and more sophisticated programs to implement the ideas he was talking about.

(Margery and Steve step forward.)

MARGERY: Good morning.

(Husband and wife nod briefly and husband continues talking as they walk by.)

HUSBAND: You see, it's all a matter of administration, sound management, and forward planning. A successful church has to be run along the lines of any other organization.

WIFE: Mmm. I see. *(Looks over her shoulder just before exiting.)* I wonder who they were?

(They exit. Margery and Steve look dejectedly after them.)

MARGERY: What's wrong with these people? Don't they realize how hard it is to stand here like a couple of stooges? What if we weren't Christians? We would doubt that God was real if we saw the people in these churches.

STEVE *(with a look of grim determination):* Well, if they don't talk to me, I'm going to talk to them!

(Two women enter, gossiping.)

WOMAN 1: Well, it was a fairly badly-done effort all around. I had to keep myself from laughing at some of the pitiful efforts at baking. I mean, if you are going to have a coffee morning, you should at least . . .

STEVE: Good morning, ladies. May I introduce myself? I'm Steve Williams and this is my wife, Margery.

(Both stop and put on sweet smiles.)

WOMAN 1: Oh, hello, how nice to have you here.

WOMAN 2: I hope you enjoyed the service.

(Margery smiles and opens her mouth to speak with them, but they resume talking, leaving Margery standing with her mouth open.)

WOMAN 1: As I was saying—Lillian walked in with the most ridiculous-looking cake. The frosting was lime green, on a banana cake!

(They exit as an old man enters, and Steve approaches him.)

STEVE: Good morning, Sir. Lovely day, isn't it? I'm Steve Williams.

OLD MAN *(eyes him closely):* Haven't seen you around here for a while.

STEVE: Uh, I've never been here before.

OLD MAN: Oh yeah? Well it's high time you started coming regular. *(Begins to shuffle off, muttering to himself.)* These young folks don't seem to come to church regular anymore. Something better to do on the Lord's Day, I suppose. Sleeping in, or racing around in one of them fancy boats. . . . *(He exits.)*

MARGERY: Steve, we've tried. Let's go home now.

STEVE: Margery, this is the seventh church we've visited in this town. I have not had one conversation at one of them. If I don't make some contact with some real Christians soon I'm going to lose my mind! I'm staying a little longer.

(Another group enters. Steve walks up and stands in their path.)

STEVE: Hello everyone. I am a visitor to your church!

(A few of them say "good morning" as they walk around him and continue their conversations.)

(Another group enters. This time Steve leaps in front of them.)

STEVE: Good morning folks! I am a visitor to your church. This is the first time I have come and I would like to meet you all!

(A few say "pleased to meet you" and they walk around him and continue on as before.)

(Another group enters. Steve leaps in front of them and spreads his arms expansively. He addresses them loudly.)

STEVE: Hello! I am new in town. My wife and I do not know a soul here and we are seeking a warm, caring fellowship to meet our needs and provide us with an avenue for service!

GROUP MEMBER: Oh, that's nice. Make sure you sign our visitors' book.

(They walk around him and exit as the other groups did. Steve is now quite beyond rational behavior. Margery has remained in the same position, sympathetically watching her husband.)

STEVE: Margery! I am going to make these people notice me if it's the last thing I do!

(He runs up to the church entrance, throws himself down on the ground about six feet away from it, sprawls out his arms and legs, closes his eyes and hangs out his tongue.)

(The minister and his wife walk out and lock the door behind them.)

MINISTER: I think we had a pretty encouraging morning. Everyone seemed to be attentive to the sermon.

MINISTER'S WIFE: They were. And your message was excellent. Very stirring.

MINISTER: Well, thank you, Dear.

(They step in unison over Steve, not looking down, seemingly oblivious of him and of Margery standing nearby.)

MINISTER: I hope it will make the members more aware of the needs of the community. I want them to see beyond the church and realize there are individuals everywhere with needs they can meet. . . .

(They exit. Steve sits up and stares after them in disbelief. Margery approaches him, eyeing him with pity. She helps him up.)

MARGERY: Come on Steve. Don't take it so badly. Maybe we'll find a friendlier bunch next week.

(They exit in silence, Steve still shaking his head in disbelief.)

Questions for Discussion

1. Have you ever felt unwelcome when you visited a church? If so, what was the cause?

2. What impression would being ignored during a first visit make on a person who was not a Christian?

3. What are the difficulties in making visitors welcome, especially in big churches?

4. How can churches be structured to make sure that everyone has the opportunity to get to know people?

5. What do you do to make visitors welcome at your church?

6. Greeting visitors, helping them find their classrooms, sitting with them in the sanctuary, etc., is part of meeting their immediate, superficial need. How can we go beyond that? What is our biggest barrier to going beyond that?

7. What, if any, responsibilities do visitors have in getting to know regulars?

8. Does our congregation suffer from cliques? Racial, social class, or religious bigotry? Do we alienate people because of their age, or marital status? Is there room for any of this in Christ's church?

A Recent Convert

When one member of a non-Christian family accepts Christ, problems can occur. It is a situation that can easily lead to lack of communication and misunderstanding. Often the Christian is teased or even persecuted, but he is sometimes guilty of escaping into the security of newfound fellowship and brushing the family aside. He may be unconcerned with the family problems, or just feel unable to communicate.

But if the family cannot see changes in attitude—more love and concern and patience, they have every reason to be skeptical about the convert's new faith. This skit illustrates a situation in which a sister's relationship with her brother has suffered by her conversion, and shows how the first steps toward restoration are made.

The skit is set in the family's living room.

Characters

Christine—seventeen to nineteen, became a Christian at a church's summer camp a few months before. She is gentle and sensitive. She and her brother are very close, but she cannot match his confidence and sarcasm in a confrontation.

Steven—A very intelligent, cynical person. He feels cut off from his sister and resents all the new Christian trappings to her life. He thinks she is being escapist.

Mother—A weak character who evades her circumstances rather than facing up to them. Her children have grown used to talking over her head.

(Christine is involved in some kind of housework or hobby that leaves her mind free [ironing, mixing cookies, knitting, etc.]. She is singing a Christian song that is pleasant, but a little too sweet. She is unaware of Steven's entrance. He stands in the doorway and listens for a moment, then startles her by speaking.)

STEVEN: That's a very sweet little song you're singing.

CHRISTINE *(turning):* I didn't hear you come in.

STEVEN *(taking a few steps into the room):* You have been singing a lot of those sweet little songs lately. Happy, banal little songs. Trite, cliched little songs.

CHRISTINE *(looking uncomfortable):* They're OK. I learn them from people at church.

STEVEN: No doubt. Along with all your new habits.

CHRISTINE *(sigh):* OK. What do you mean?

STEVEN: Well, there are your new friends who you spend no less than two hours a night talking to on the phone— every evening—usually in subdued, secretive tones. I overheard you yesterday though—asking one of them to pray for me.

(Christine winces.)

Then there's church, twice on Sunday. And you leave at some ungodly hour on that day of rest so you can catch your morning Bible class. Not to mention the mid-week prayer meeting. . .

CHRISTINE *(cuts in, trying to explain):* I asked Carolyn to pray for you only because you are so tired and uptight. I didn't go into your personal life or anything . . .

STEVEN: . . . I'm not finished yet. We can't forget all the avid Bible reading and the verses stuck up on your bedroom

93

wall. You used to read classics and poetry and philosophy. Now all I see around are sappy little "How to have a wonderful life" books. My baby sister is a fanatic.

(He sits down on a chair or couch. He has succeeded in intimidating her, but she makes an effort to make him understand.)

CHRISTINE: Maybe, maybe it looks like I am going overboard. But I've finally found something true and I want to get into it as much as I can.

STEVEN: So you have found universal truth! That elusive discovery denied lesser men like me who don't go in for summer church camps.

CHRISTINE *(getting upset):* You don't talk to me for weeks and then you finally break the silence with a string of insults. What's the matter with you? Why don't you just cut out the sarcastic crap?

STEVEN *(smiles):* Crap? Crap? Christians don't say crap. They say "nonsense," or "piffle."

CHRISTINE *(shaking her head):* I thought you would be happy that I'm happy. We used to talk so much about how to be happy and not mess up like Mom and Dad and when I find out how, and want to tell you, you just cut me right off. You treat me like I died last week.

STEVEN: Christine, you *think* you are happy. You are really just bombing out. You're into a cozy system that dishes up all the answers and you have decided to hide in it. You're as bad as Mom reading her romantic novels and going shopping all the time—just another form of escapism. You've always had that tendency. You always were a little dreamy.

CHRISTINE *(after a pause):* Well, go on. It used to take you a lot longer to tell me why I do things.

STEVEN: No need in this case. It's that simple.

CHRISTINE *(trying again to get through):* You don't know what I believe. You don't know if it's valid. You haven't been talking to me since I got back. You hardly ever come home anymore.

STEVEN: *I* haven't been talking to *you*? What am I supposed to do? Catch you in between church services? What do you need to talk to me for when you have all these wonderful, new caring friends?

(Christine shows surprise. For the first time she realizes that part of the distance between them is her fault. Mother enters, paperback in her hand.)

MOTHER: Oh, hello Steven. You're home. How are you? How's school?

STEVEN: Mom, I'm doing my honors year in psychology. It's time you started calling it university.

MOTHER: Well, you know what I mean. *(Sits in a chair, book poised.)* I heard you raising your voice just now. Is anything the matter?

STEVEN: Oh no. *(Looking at Christine.)* Christine and I were just having a pleasant discussion.

CHRISTINE *(looking back):* Oh, I don't know about that.

MOTHER: You're not picking on your sister again are you? I thought you two had stopped arguing lately. *(Starts reading.)*

STEVEN: We weren't arguing, we were talking about the meaning of life. Christine is now well acquainted with it.

CHRISTINE *(pleads):* Please stop it Steven. I don't want to fight with you. I don't want to annoy you. I'm sorry if I annoy you.

MOTHER *(turning a page):* There Steven, look how nicely she apologizes now. Stop being mean.

STEVEN: Why don't you tell your mother and me something about the meaning of life, Christine? I'm sure we both need to know.

(Mother looks up from her book.)

CHRISTINE *(decides to take him seriously):* Well, we were made to live for God. He made us with something in mind—for a reason.

STEVEN: OK. We've got the meaning of life straight. Now tell us what our morals are supposed to be.

MOTHER: Oh Steven. *(Starts reading again.)*

CHRISTINE *(chooses her words carefully):* We're supposed to live with the benefit of the other person in mind. You have to start ignoring the impulse to always do what you want.

STEVEN: I was thinking more specifically of the area of sexual morality.

(Mother looks up sharply.)

CHRISTINE: You're not supposed to separate sex from love. And you are not supposed to sleep with someone until you've made a lifetime commitment to her, if that's what you are getting at.

MOTHER: This is a ridiculous conversation. I can see I am going to have to go somewhere else to get some peace and quiet. *(She exits.)*

STEVEN *(speaking more rapidly):* Now, tell me Christine, does the devil exist?

CHRISTINE: Yes, but probably not the way you imagine him.

STEVEN: Tell me then, why is it that God puts up with the devil. Couldn't he just get rid of him?

CHRISTINE: Yes, I guess. Oh, I don't know. Steven, that's a bit heavy to throw out like a quiz show question. That's too hard for me to understand right away.

STEVEN: Oh, so you just accept it. Let's talk about Jesus then. He is the one you are supposed to be eternally indebted to. He died for us, is that right? As we were told in Sunday school?

CHRISTINE *(dejected now):* Yes.

STEVEN: And God knew all about His death and had it all planned?

CHRISTINE: Yes.

STEVEN: Yes. But I can't help thinking about poor old Judas. Was he part of the plan too? The inevitable stooge; ends justifying means, so to speak?

CHRISTINE *(close to tears):* Oh Steven—we can't talk about it like this! These are deep issues and I don't know everything yet. You're just trying to trip me up.

STEVEN *(angry, stands up and moves nearer to her):* Well, just tell me this one thing, then, and I'll leave you alone. Just tell me where God is. What's He doing while little kids are getting beat up by their parents and women are getting bombed while they go shopping? All those things are happening while you sit in church. And where was He last week when John got creamed off his motorcycle? *(Christine looks down.)* And what does He think about the way people like us live? Why, at this very moment your father is probably off with his secretary while your mother reads her fourth romance novel this week!

CHRISTINE *(covering her face with her hands):* Stop it! Stop it!

(He stops, ashamed. Runs a hand through his hair.)

STEVEN: I'm sorry. You didn't deserve that. I even scare myself sometimes. I'm sorry.

CHRISTINE: I'm not explaining it to you right. I keep imagining all the ways I could get across to you what I'm learning because it is so important but I can never quite say it and you pick up on all the wrong things. The main part is just what God is like and what He has done and what He wants you to do. . . . I feel like you don't like me anymore.

STEVEN *(speaking more quietly)*: You've changed. You can't see things on my level anymore.

CHRISTINE: I know. . . . But I like you more than I used to.

STEVEN *(intrigued)*: What do you mean?

CHRISTINE: I do. Now that I am not so unhappy and worried about myself I am starting to think about you more.

STEVEN: Think what?

CHRISTINE: How you are basically depressed all the time. You have too many things weighing you down and you are disillusioned with everyone even though you try to care about people.

(She rises and walks a few steps away from him.)

The reason I can't talk to you very well anymore is that it is more important for me to talk to you now. So I'm hung up about it.

STEVEN *(for once at a loss as to what to say)*: Well, what would you tell me if you could?

CHRISTINE: Well, I am worried about you. *(She faces him again.)* Not in a self-righteous way, but because I am seeing how there is only one thing worth living for and I am afraid you will not find it. . . . I can't get it across to you in any way you would not be immune to. . . . Except if you read the Bible for yourself maybe.

STEVEN: I don't think so Christine.

CHRISTINE: Just a Gospel then. They're not long. It wouldn't kill you.

STEVEN: And you think that's going to make me a Christian?

CHRISTINE: Probably not. But you might start thinking differently. You might see that there's something to it and that I'm not as stupid as you think.

STEVEN *(smiles):* It would make you feel better would it—me reading some of the Bible?

CHRISTINE: Yes. I can give you one without the "thees" and "thous" in it.

STEVEN: Whatever. OK then. I guess I can make a little effort to fathom all this newfound truth of yours. I'll read your Bible. All I can say is that it better be good.

Questions for Discussion

1. Why was this conversation significant? What was accomplished?

2. In what ways might Steven have been justified in his criticism of Christine?

3. If you were in Christine's position, how would you have responded to Steven's questions about life's meaning, morals, the gospel, and suffering?

4. How did Christine show that a new Christian can witness effectively even before she has gathered a lot of Biblical knowledge?

5. How can a new Christian illustrate that her faith is a good thing to a skeptical family? How should she behave and not behave?

6. What responsibility does the church have towards members from unbelieving families? How can Christian friends help in this situation?

7. A common criticism of Christians is that they hide from the evils of the world behind a dreamy, pie-in-the sky philosophy. How valid is this criticism?

8. New Christian or old, Peter instructs us to "be ready always to give an answer to every man that asketh you a reason of the hope that is in you" (1 Peter 3:15). How can we achieve this readiness? How much of that readiness has to do with attitude? willingness? fear? knowledge?

9. How can we take our faith beyond the realm of philosophy and into the real and practical world? What effect would this have on unbelievers?

Missionaries Are Real People Too

To many people, the word "missionary" conjures up a totally unrealistic image. People outside the church often have negative opinions of missionaries, and many people in the church are quite ignorant of what those in cross-cultural ministries are actually facing.

This skit proposes to show how ridiculous the stereotypes are. It would be ideal for presentation with a report of what is happening on the mission field. The three interviews that make up the skit can be alternated with serious narrations to provide a light touch and a dramatic contrast.

The skit consists of three encounters between a mission team and people who have volunteered to come help them. The volunteers display the stereotyped personalities that people too often imagine when they think of missionaries.

The setting is a living room, arranged for an interviewing process. There is a table set in the middle of the room with two chairs behind it for the missionary couple and one chair in front for the volunteers. The third member of the mission team will move from chair to couch to pace the floor, etc. The volunteers will enter and exit from door to the living room.

The success of this skit will lie in how much the volunteer workers can exaggerate their characters and how well the mission team can communicate what they are thinking by use of their expressions, voice inflections, and exchanged looks.

Characters

Robert and Carol—a middle-aged, married couple who have been on the mission field for thirty years. They are calm, dedicated, and intelligent.

Ben—an unmarried co-worker on the mission team. His enthusiasm and dedication to his work sometime override his good sense.

Jenny—Robert and Carol's teenage daughter who acts as their secretary.

Nigel Forsythe—wants to be the great, white hunter. Sees missionaries as battling their way through the jungle and having great adventures.

Miss Higginbothom—an exuberant but petty, self-righteous lady who wants to go and tame the savages.

William Formidable—a solemn, legalistic preacher who spouts cliches and understands little about people.

(Robert and Carol are seated at the table, doing some paperwork. Ben enters, hands some papers to Robert, and sits near the table.)

ROBERT: Are these the letters from the people who are coming this morning?

BEN: Yeah, we got quite a few responses to the requests for more workers, and some of them look pretty good. One of the women coming this morning is a nurse, and one of the men is a minister.

CAROL: That's exciting! With the start we've made in South Africa, more workers could really get things rolling.

BEN: Don't get your hopes up too high. Remember, these are first enquiries. You know what kind of oddballs we can get.

Remember the guy who wanted to work as a missionary for a few months as a tax dodge—asked us to send him to the Greek Islands?

ROBERT: Yeah. But maybe we'll get some serious ones today.

(He barely finishes speaking when a loud "What ho!" is heard offstage, followed by the sound of running feet. A zealous-looking man in a safari suit and pith helmet charges on stage, bounds across to the team and surveys all around him with an air of attack.)

NIGEL FORSYTHE: Good day chaps! I say, are you the ones seeking assistance in the mission field?

(The mission team is momentarily stupefied, in thinly disguised shock.)

ROBERT *(trying to compose himself):* Yes, yes we are. You must be Nigel Forsythe. Take a seat, Mr. Forsythe.

FORSYTHE: Oh perhaps not old chap, *(Nods to Carol.)* Madam, thanks just the same. I'd rather stand. Usually do, you know. *(Saunters around the front of the stage, pauses on the opposite side of the team).*

FORSYTHE: I say, you wouldn't be looking for someone to go to the African jungle would you?

ROBERT: Why do you ask?

FORSYTHE: Well, I think I'd do marvelously well out there, you know, all those great adventures and what not; killing lions with my bare hands *(Strangling gesture.),* saving white women from cannibals, diverting elephant stampedes—that sort of thing. I think. . . .

BEN *(interrupts)* : I think you'd better sit down.

(Subdued by Ben's voice, Forsythe sits in chair provided.)

ROBERT: In your letter, you were very vague about your professional abilities, and your training. We obviously have to make sure that the people we recruit are not only committed to the Lord, we have to know where and how they may be most helpful. The occupation you've listed here is especially bewildering. *(Consults a form.)* What exactly does, "Enrichment of the human mind and the advancement of technology" mean?

FORSYTHE *(reluctantly):* Well, um, it sort of means I'm, well, I sell computer games in a toy store.

CAROL: Well there's nothing wrong with that Mr. Forsythe, except that you should have stated it plainly.

FORSYTHE: I know. But it isn't very exciting. I'd much rather be stalking tigers.

(The missionaries give one another dubious looks.)

ROBERT: You didn't mention anything about your Bible training, or involvement in Christian work. Could you give us some details there?

FORSYTHE: Oh yes. Training. *(Pause.)* Well, I've always gone to church, so there's no problems with all the Christian business, you know.

BEN *(fairly disturbed by now):* Excuse me, Mr. Forsythe. Could you tell me where you learned about missionaries? When did you first believe you were called to this life in the African jungle?

FORSYTHE *(assumes melodramatic expression, moves away from the team, puts hand to heart and stares into the distance):* Ever since I was nine years old, I have known. Ever since those first Saturday matinees when I observed those brave men of God, fighting their way through the dense undergrowth in search of the unsaved. I've always known that this was the life for me.

BEN *(exasperated):* Then maybe you'd better buy a ticket to L.A. and do a screen test for Universal Studios. This is cross-cultural missionary work, not Adventureland!

FORSYTHE *(unabashed):* Oh. Well old chap, if you should happen to change your mind, you know where to contact me. Remember now, the African jungle. . . .

(Carol shows him to the door as he speaks, then turns, stunned, back to her colleagues.)

CAROL: Did that really happen? Did a man actually come in here wearing a pith helmet and ask us to send him to the African jungle?

ROBERT *(shaking his head):* I think the best thing to do is quickly move on to the next volunteer. She is probably a sensible, matronly woman who is just the sort of helper we need.

INTERVIEW 2

CAROL *(calls out of the room):* Jenny, is Miss Higginbothom here yet?

JENNY *(offstage):* Yes Mom, she is.

CAROL: Send her in now, please.

(Miss Higginbothom bustles in, wearing old fashioned, sensible clothes and shoes, but a ridiculous hat. Everyone says "good morning.")

HIGGINBOTHOM: Good morning.

ROBERT: Please sit down. We're glad that you could manage to come and speak with us on your day off.

HIGGINBOTHOM: Well, I have just finished baking cookies for the church bazaar and I will have to leave rather soon in order to attend a local Christian Ladies' Charity and the Good Works Organization's embroidery session—but, I wanted to speak with you because I really think it's time I did become a missionary, because I can no longer endure the shocking state of affairs in those native villages!

BEN: Uh, which native villages?

HIGGINBOTHOM *(baffled)* : Well, all of them!

CAROL: Are you speaking of poverty?

HIGGINBOTHOM: Poverty? Yes, but what horrifies me most is their immorality and their uncivilized living habits!

BEN: Do you have a burden for any particular people out of all the world's population who inhabit "native villages"?

HIGGINBOTHOM: Yes. The Godless savages in Papua, New Guinea.

(The team shows shock at her terminology.)

ROBERT: Miss Higginbothom! I see from your letter that you are a nurse. Supposing you did go to a clinic in a village in Papua, New Guinea. How do you think you could get close to the people and minister to them. What would be the first thing you would do?

HIGGINBOTHOM: Well! I have no doubts on that score. Before anything else could be done, I would put decent clothes on all those topless, heathen women! *(Crosses her arms with self-righteous resolve.)*

BEN: Miss Higginbothom, I don't want to discourage you, but you've missed the point. You would not be going to teach the dress habits of western culture or impose your moral code. You would go to show people Jesus Christ. Are you willing to do that? Do you see the need for patience and love and respect for any people?

HIGGINBOTHOM: Of course. But first things first. You can't go to a Bible study before you put clothes on. I intend only to demonstrate proper standards to these people.

CAROL: Did you read the literature we sent you?

HIGGINBOTHOM: Well I must confess I have had more pressing duties than reading pamphlets.

ROBERT: Perhaps you ought to go home and think things over a little more, read the pamphlets, and pray about it before you contact us again.

HIGGINBOTHOM *(offended):* Oh, I see. Very well. Perhaps my abilities *will* be better appreciated elsewhere. Thank you for your time. I can show myself out.

(She bustles out as the team tries to say good-bye. After she leaves, Robert and Carol can't help smiling. Ben sits shaking his head in disbelief.)

BEN: What is this, Candid Camera?

ROBERT: I need a cup of coffee. I cannot risk continuing this until I have a cup of coffee. *(Calls out to the other room.)* Could you come in Jenny? *(Jenny enters almost immediately.)* Do you think you could bring us some coffee?

JENNY: Sure, but, um, I was wondering if maybe you could see the minister pretty soon. He's been here fifteen minutes.

CAROL: Oh, he's way too early for his appointment—is he in a hurry?

JENNY: I don't know, but he makes me kind of nervous. He won't talk or anything. He just sits there, with a creepy, solemn expression.

ROBERT *(sighs):* Well, let's get it over with. We'll have the coffee after.

JENNY: Oh, what a relief. Thanks.

(She exits.)

INTERVIEW 3

(Enter William Formidable, dressed in a severe, black suit, stiff white shirt, black tie. He is very solemn, and carries a large black Bible. He nods in response to their greetings and they all sit down. There is an awkward pause because his mere presence creates an uncomfortable atmosphere. Ben ventures to speak first.)

BEN: We were pleased to receive your letter, Mr. Formidable.

(No reply. Another awkward pause.)

ROBERT: I see from your letter that you are interested in working with the South American Indians—the Bolivians. Could you tell us why? What made you want to . . .

FORMIDABLE *(stands suddenly, arm raised):* The day of the Lord is upon us! It approaches like a thief in the night . . . we are commanded to preach the gospel to every tribe and every nation, to the ends of the earth . . . Jesus stands at the door and knocks . . . *(His volume is increasing as he preaches, the missionaries are looking at one another in amazement.)*

ROBERT: Uh, excuse me—*(Formidable pays no attention.)*

FORMIDABLE: . . . If any man hears His voice and opens the door . . .

BEN: Mr. Formidable—

FORMIDABLE: . . . the Lord will come in and eat with him . . .

BEN *(more sharply):* Mr. Formidable! *(Formidable finally hears, stops and looks at him.)* We already know that! We are trying to establish whether or not you'll be able to get it across to people who don't. *(He pauses while Formidable sits down.)* As a church leader for over twenty years, you are obviously—experienced—in preaching to people of your own culture. You say you're interested in the Bolivian Indians. Have you learned about their lifestyles, their religions.

FORMIDABLE *(leaning forward):* You mean their idolatry! They worship only false gods. Given over to the powers of darkness, subject to every kind of evil. They must be warned! It will not be on my head if they are eternally lost!

BEN: What would saving them involve?

FORMIDABLE: Why that's obvious—crusades, evangelistic meetings in every town and village. Distribution of tracts and New Testaments!

CAROL: What if they can't read?

FORMIDABLE *(pause):* Oh, well, some will be able to. They can tell the others.

ROBERT: If, and we are speaking hypothetically, if some accepted Christ after a whirlwind crusade, what would they do after you had gone to the next place?

FORMIDABLE: Go to church, live godly lives, free themselves from all hatred, malice, greed, immorality. . . .

BEN *(interrupts):* What if there are no churches, no one to teach them, no Christians living among them?

FORMIDABLE *(pauses):* I see. The situation could be rather difficult, couldn't it?

BEN *(angry):* Difficult, yes. A little. I would have thought that after twenty years in the ministry, you would realize what is involved in changing a person's heart. The months or years or decades it takes, and the understanding. And you should know that conversion is hardly the end of the story, or the end of your work among a group of people.

(The other team members are uncomfortable at the outburst. They try to smooth things over.)

ROBERT: Uh, what I think he means to say, Mr. Formidable, is that weekend crusades don't quite do the trick.

FORMIDABLE: Are you saying I would have to spend some time with these people?

CAROL: Yes, that's what we're saying.

FORMIDABLE: I suppose I shall have to think more about this. Perhaps I'll contact you at a later date. Good-bye.

(He exits.)

ROBERT *(to Ben):* That was a pretty useless outburst.

BEN: I know. I'm sorry for it. But three in a row like that makes you ready to throw in the towel.

ROBERT: Don't be so dramatic. They're leftovers from the past. Let's have our coffee now.

Questions for Discussion

1. Discuss the motive of each person who volunteered to be a missionary. In what ways were their attitudes unrealistic and unhelpful?

2. How successful would each of them have been if they had actually gone to a mission field?

3. What do you think of when you hear the word, "missionary"?

4. How informed are you about Christian work in other countries?

5. Is it important for Christians to be informed about world missions? Why?

6. What can we do, as individuals and as churches, to be more informed and supportive of Christian work among other cultures?

7. Like Miss Higginbothom, many people confuse cultural standards and social standards with God's standards. How does this interfere with sharing the gospel, even among people in the same city?